Bahá'í Children's Classes
and Retreats: Theme #5

The Power of Unity

Dr. Randie S. Gottlieb

Published by
UnityWorks LLC

The Power of Unity
Teacher's Guide with Lesson Plans for Ages 8-12

ISBN 978-0-9828979-5-9

© 2010 UnityWorks LLC. First edition 2005 (spiral bound)
Second printing 2012

All rights reserved. No part of this book may be reproduced or transmitted in any form or by any means without prior written permission from the publisher.

UnityWorks hereby grants permission for one children's class teacher or Bahá'í school to copy student handouts as needed. Handouts are also available for downloading from: www.UnityWorksStore.com.

The small fee charged for our materials helps to cover printing costs, the development of new products, and the maintenance of our website to make these resources more widely available. If you find these items useful, please let others know about them. Thank you!

Available from: www.UnityWorksStore.com

Quotations from the Bahá'í writings reprinted with permission of
the National Spiritual Assembly of the Bahá'ís of the United States
and the Bahá'í Publishing Trust of Wilmette, IL.

Special thanks to my husband, Steven E. Gottlieb, M.D.
for his support and editorial assistance.

Appreciation to Jordan Gottlieb for assistance
with the cover design and pre-press work.

Cover illustration, Kamal Siegel
Back cover artwork courtesy of: www.clipsahoy.com

Remaining clip art images taken or adapted from:
The Big Box of Art from www.Hemera.com

All websites and references listed
are correct at the time of publication.

Published by UnityWorks, LLC
www.UnityWorksStore.com
Yakima, Washington, USA

Dedicated to the Morphet-Brown Family
Ken, Mary, Ben, Jesse and Augustin

For their loving example of unity
and courage over the years

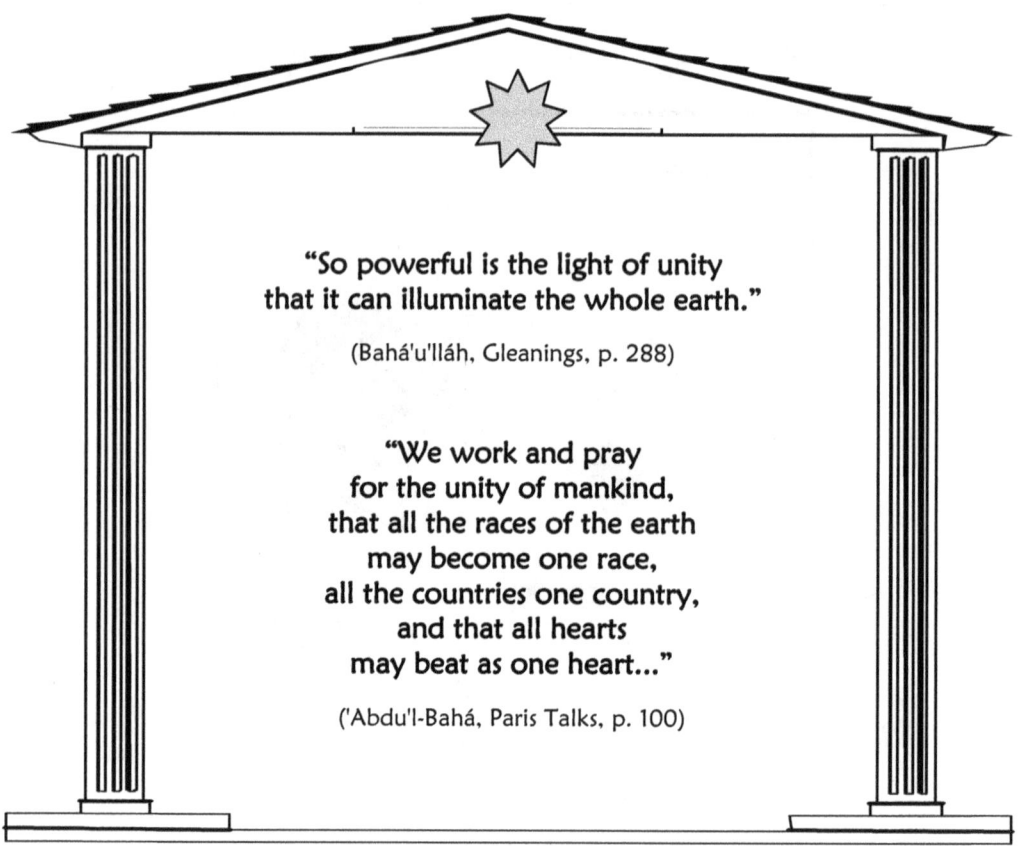

"So powerful is the light of unity
that it can illuminate the whole earth."

(Bahá'u'lláh, Gleanings, p. 288)

"We work and pray
for the unity of mankind,
that all the races of the earth
may become one race,
all the countries one country,
and that all hearts
may beat as one heart..."

('Abdu'l-Bahá, Paris Talks, p. 100)

The Power of Unity

TABLE OF CONTENTS

Introduction	1
Overview	2
To the Organizers	4
Teachers	4
Special Role of Youth	4
Schedule	5
Handouts	5
Sample Retreat Flyer with Registration Form	6
Sample Retreat Schedules	7
To the Teacher	10
Opening Activities and Orientation Program	13

LESSONS

1. The Power of Unity	21
2. Unity in Diversity	33
3. The Colors We Are	57
4. Overcoming Prejudice	73
Additional Activities	97
Children's Performance	125
Handouts	141
Song Sheet	143
Quotations	145
The Power of Unity	147
Music	161
Closing Activities and Follow-up	179
References for Teachers	183
Bibliography	207
Works by the Same Author	209
List of Activities by Chapter	213
Index of Activities by Category	217

The Power of Unity

INTRODUCTION

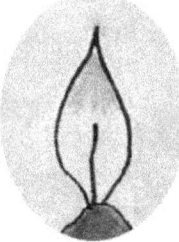

Bahá'u'lláh has prescribed unto all people, "that which will lead to the exaltation of the Word of God amongst His servants, and likewise, to the advancement of the world of being." "To this end," He states, "the greatest means is education of the child."[1]

"My highest wish and desire," proclaims 'Abdu'l-Bahá, "is that ye who are my children may be educated according to the teachings of Bahá'u'lláh...that ye may each become a lighted candle in the world of humanity."[2] He adds that we should "let them make the greatest progress in the shortest span of time."[3]

The Universal House of Justice has likewise called upon us to involve Bahá'í children in "programmes of activity that will engage their interests [and] mold their capacities for teaching and service."[4]

The International Teaching Centre has affirmed that "these young people should then be seen as a door to entry by troops and as a fruitful source of teachers...not simply as children for whom activity must be arranged...but as a living creation of God necessary at this very moment for the purposes of God..."[5]

The purpose of these classes, then, is to systematically familiarize children with the fundamental truths of the Bahá'í Revelation, and to increase their desire and capacity to teach and serve. Additional goals are to strengthen bonds of friendship, and to provide an enjoyable Bahá'í activity which children will enthusiastically look forward to and invite their friends.
In the words of some participants:

"Wow! I love the subject matter—the Power of Unity—it speaks across lines of race, religion, gender and all the other divisions that we use to separate ourselves. Really wonderful work." (Beth Shevin)

"A human being cannot describe how much you guys did for me. Thank you from the bottom of my heart." (Zia, age 11)

"I love the great variety of approaches. Parents impressed and happy! THANK YOU!" (Lani Diessner)

"It would be great if all kids could have these same Bahá'í lessons." (Tiara Urlacher, youth volunteer)

References

1. Bahá'í Education: A Compilation, p. 4
2. Selections from the Writings of 'Abdu'l-Bahá, p. 141
3. Bahá'í Education: A Compilation, p. 71
4. Ridván 2000 Message
5. To the Boards of Counselors, 5 Dec. 1988

The Power of Unity

OVERVIEW

TEACHER'S GUIDES FOR CHILDREN'S CLASSES

It is hoped that this easy-to-use teacher's guide, the fifth in a series for the Bahá'í education of children, will be a useful resource for Bahá'í summer and winter schools, Holy Day programs and weekend retreats. It might also be included in a parent's toolkit for home schooling, or form part of the religious curriculum for a full-time Baha'i-inspired academic school—such as the one our family established in Puerto Rico where many of these lessons were developed.

Anticipating future needs, with a few minor modifications, some of the theme books might also be appropriate for upper elementary public school classrooms. "The Manifestation of God," for example, would be well-suited for a class on comparative religion, and "The Power of Unity," could offer a valuable contribution to a unit on diversity and the oneness of humankind.

Each book is filled with fun, hands-on, kid-tested learning activities designed for ages 8-12. These activities were developed and tested in the field, in response to the needs of teachers and children, and have been used successfully in multiple settings over many years.

The lessons incorporate a variety of instructional strategies as recommended in the Bahá'í Writings on education, such as learning through play, questioning, memorization, consultation, reflection, stories, speeches, music, arts and crafts, science, independent investigation, lectures, group discussion, plays and recreational activities.

When used as part of an intensive program, such as a summer school or weekend retreat, the teacher will need to select activities to fit within the time allotted. If the lessons are part of an ongoing program such as a daily or weekly academic class, one or more activities can be selected for each session, until the entire course has been completed. Utilized in this way, there is sufficient material in each book for several months of weekly classes.

The lessons are user-friendly and ready-to-go with very little outside preparation needed by the teacher. Essentially everything is included, with the exception of craft supplies and common household items. Each book has a sample retreat schedule, detailed lesson plans, instructions and patterns for making classroom materials, copy-ready student handouts, song sheets, music, and plans for a children's performance. When optional materials are recommended (e.g., photographs or videos), the sources are given.

The Power of Unity

Each teacher's guide focuses on a distinct theme, with all of the lessons, songs, crafts and other learning activities integrated around that theme. The series includes:

(1) GOD AND THE UNIVERSE
- The Kingdoms of Creation
- God, the Creator
- Prayer, Our Connection with God
- What Is a Human Being?

(2) THE MANIFESTATION
- Station of the Manifestation
- Introduction to the Prophets
- Progressive Revelation
- One Common Faith

(3) THE BÁB: GATE TO BAHÁ'U'LLÁH
- His Birth and Early Life
- Declaration of the Báb
- Martyrdom of the Báb
- The Primal Point

(4) BAHÁ'U'LLÁH: THE GLORY OF GOD
- His Birth, Early Life and Station
- Declaration of Bahá'u'lláh
- Exiles and Imprisonment
- Clouds of Glory

(5) THE POWER OF UNITY
- The Power of Unity
- Unity in Diversity
- The Colors We Are
- Overcoming Prejudice

Additional theme books are being prepared on 'Abdu'l-Bahá, Bahá'í Principles, Bahá'í Laws and Institutions, Consultation for Kids, and The Bahá'í Community.

CHILDREN'S RETREAT PLANNING GUIDE

These theme books can be used in conjunction with the *Bahá'í Children's Retreat Planning Guide,* which is available from www.UnityWorksStore.com. It covers the following topics:

- ❏ Scheduling
- ❏ Sponsorship
- ❏ Participants
- ❏ Teachers
- ❏ Other volunteers
- ❏ Facility
- ❏ Publicity
- ❏ Finances
- ❏ Pre-registration
- ❏ Materials
- ❏ Site preparation
- ❏ Sample schedule
- ❏ On-site registration
- ❏ Orientation
- ❏ Outdoor activities
- ❏ Children's performance
- ❏ Closing activities
- ❏ Food, forms, signs

The Power of Unity

TO THE ORGANIZERS

Teachers

This teacher's guide includes four lessons on *The Power of Unity*. One individual could teach all four lessons; the classes can be team-taught; or a different person might be asked to lead each class.

Special Role of Youth

Capable youth and junior youth can be invited to assist with the classes and activities. We have found that many former participants are eager to return to the children's retreats as volunteers. Inspired by this experience, a high percentage of them have gone on to complete junior youth animator training, and several have arisen to organize children's classes or junior youth groups in their home communities.

The participation of youth volunteers at the retreat is also a great help for the adults and a joy for the younger children, while offering the youth an opportunity to apply their institute training and to acquire new skills. The youth are given guided experience and hands-on teaching practice. They return home with new confidence, encouraged and motivated to support local children's classes in their own neighborhoods. In addition, a wonderful community atmosphere is created with all age groups working together to educate the children.

In the words of one youth:

> *"The retreats have been an integral part of my growing up experience, and I'm so grateful for the opportunity to come and help out now as a youth. It's really special to see my brothers and cousins and their friends, and know that they'll grow up with the same wonderful friendships and learning experiences and shared memories that my generation of youth gained.*
>
> *"I learned a lot about myself and discovered how to help kids learn and grow, and ways to make their experience happy. Although I went through all the same lessons myself, it's still great to hear and see the lessons again. Us kids have <u>so</u> much fun every time and I am always looking forward to the next retreat."* (Brynne Haug, age 16)

Youth volunteers: Kierra, Yuri, Alonso, Layli, Alex, Brynne, Carew

Schedule

If planning a weekend retreat, the lessons can be scheduled over a two-day or a three-day period. Sample schedules for both are included below. The two-day schedule offers participants a choice of some of the crafts and activities. The three-day schedule includes more of the crafts and classroom activities, additional time for memorization practice, an evening talent show, and a group consultation on how to share with others the concepts learned at the retreat. For an ongoing class, all of the activities can be included.

Handouts

Some handouts are included with the lessons, while others have been grouped near the end of this book for convenience in photocopying. They can also be downloaded from: **www.UnityWorksStore.com** (click on Children's Classes > The Power of Unity > student handouts). The handouts can be copied one at a time as needed for a particular class, or all at once as part of the handout packet for a summer school or weekend retreat.

The **Schedule, Songs** and **Quotations** should be photocopied for all participants and included in their folders during registration. If each item is copied on paper of a different color, it will be easier for the children to find. The songs and quotations should each be copied on two sides of the page to save paper and for ease of use.

The 13-page packet on *The Power of Unity* (from the title sheet through *Creating Unity*) should be copied back-to-back on white paper, stapled together and included in the folders. This packet will be used in various lessons.

Each instructor should be given **To the Teacher** (pages 10-12), a copy of the appropriate lesson plan, and **References for Teachers** (found at the end of this book), along with the handouts mentioned above. Teachers should also make copies of any additional handouts needed for their specific lessons.

The coordinator of the children's performance will need copies of the entire **Children's Performance** section (pages 125-139), in addition to the schedule, song sheet, page of quotations, and the "Power of Unity" handout packet.

The song leader will need **To the Music Coordinator** and copies of each song, found in the section on music (pages 160-176).

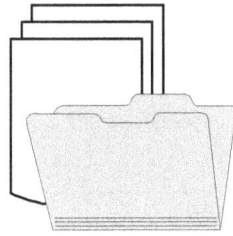

The Power of Unity

— Sample Flyer —

BAHÁ'Í CHILDREN'S RETREAT #5
Sponsored by the Bahá'ís of Our Town

KIDS: AGES 8 –12

THEME: The Power of Unity

Join us for a fun weekend of Bahá'í classes, prayers, singing, arts & crafts, archery, games, storytelling, tasty food & more!

> **May 6-8**
> *Noorani Home, 1919 Unity Lane*
> *Our Town, WA 98765 - (919) 765-4321*

COST: $35 per child or $30 if paid before April 6. Additional children from same family, $20 each. Scholarships available. Make checks payable to: Bahá'ís of Our Town. Space is limited, apply now!

Participants should bring: sleeping bag, pillow, towel, toothbrush and paste, comb, any medicines with clear instructions, bathing suit, sturdy shoes, pajamas and change of clothes. Please do NOT bring: electronic games, radios, CDs, iPods, etc.

> *Starts Friday at 5:30 p.m. with registration and dinner. Ends at 2:00 p.m. on Sunday*

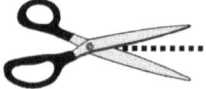 ··

BAHÁ'Í CHILDREN'S RETREAT

Mail this form to: Lua Smith, 1863 Ridván Lane, Our Town, WA 98765
Email: lsmith@gmail.com - Tel: (919) 123-4567

Child's name (print): _____ Age: _____ Sex: _____

Address: _____ Phone: _____

Email: _____ Fee enclosed: $ _____ Partial scholarship requested: $ _____

Emergency contact: _____ Phone: _____

Medical or dietary information: _____

The child named above has my permission to attend the Bahá'í Children's Retreat on May 6-8, 2011, at the Noorani home in Our Town. I understand that s/he is participating at her/his own risk. If necessary, I hereby give the event organizers permission to administer first aid and obtain emergency medical treatment.

_____   _____   _____
Parent or Guardian (print name)   Signature   Date

Bahá'í Children's Retreat

Noorani home, Our Town, May 6-8, 2011

"The Power of Unity"

FRIDAY
- 5:30 pm — Registration, decorate folders
- 6:00 — Dinner
- 7:30 — Prayers, singing, orientation
- **8:00 — Evening program**
- 9:00 — Volunteer briefing
- 9:30 — Group song, prayers and bedtime
- 10:00 — Lights out

SATURDAY
- 7:30 am — Morning prayers
- 8:00 — Breakfast
- 8:30 — Singing
- **8:45 — Class #1: The Power of Unity** (75 min.)
- 10:00 — Break
- **10:30 — Class #2: Unity in Diversity** (1 hr. 45 min.)
- 12:15 pm — Lunch and quiet time
- **1:30 — Class #3: The Colors We Are** (90 min.)
- 3:00 — Snack and outdoor activities
- 4:30 — Rehearsal for evening program
- 6:00 — Dinner
- 7:00 — Prepare refreshments, rehearse songs
- **8:00 — Evening program**
- 9:15 — Refreshments and socializing
- 10:00 — Group song, prayers and bedtime
- 10:30 — Lights out

SUNDAY
- 8:00 am — Morning prayers
- 8:30 — Breakfast
- 9:00 — Singing
- **9:15 — Class #4: Overcoming Prejudice** (1 hr. 45 min.)
- 11:00 — Outdoor activities
- 12:00 pm — Lunch
- 12:30 — Clean-up
- 1:00 — Closing activities, evaluation, graduation
- 1:30 — Group photo
- 1:45 — Dessert
- 2:00 — Check lost-and-found; farewells

The Power of Unity

— Sample **3-Day** Schedule —

Bahá'í Children's Retreat

Noorani home, Our Town, May 6-8, 2011

"The Power of Unity"

FRIDAY
5:30 pm	Registration, decorate folders
6:00	Dinner
7:30	Prayers, singing, orientation
8:00	**Evening program**
9:00	Volunteer briefing
9:30	Group song, prayers and bedtime
10:00	Lights out

SATURDAY
7:30 am	Morning prayers
8:00	Breakfast
8:30	Singing
8:45	**Class #1: The Power of Unity** (75 min.)
10:00	Break
10:30	**Class #2: Unity in Diversity** (1 hr. 45 min.)
12:15 pm	Lunch and quiet time
1:30	Craft activities
3:00	Snack and outdoor activities
4:30	Memorization practice (alone, pairs or groups)
5:15	Group singing practice or free time
6:00	Dinner
7:30	Singing and share memorized quotes
8:15	Evening snack
8:30	Evening program (Bahá'í video, talent show, etc.)
9:30	Group song, prayers and bedtime
10:00	Lights out

SUNDAY
8:00 am	Morning prayers
8:30	Breakfast
9:00	Singing
9:15	**Class #3: The Colors We Are** (90 min.)
10:45	Outdoor activities
12:00 pm	Lunch and quiet time
1:30	**Class #4: Overcoming Prejudice** (1 hr. 45 min.)
3:15	Snack and outdoor activities
4:15	Rehearsal for evening program
6:00	Dinner

The Power of Unity

— Sample **3-Day** Schedule, continued —

SUNDAY
7:00 pm   Prepare refreshments, rehearse songs
8:00   **Evening program**
9:15   Refreshments and socializing
10:00   Group song, prayers and bedtime
10:30   Lights out

MONDAY
8:30 am   Morning prayers
9:00   Breakfast
9:30   Singing
9:45   **Group consultation on how to share what we learned**
10:30   Outdoor activities
12:00 pm   Lunch
12:30   Clean-up
1:00   Closing activities, evaluation, graduation
1:30   Group photo
1:45   Dessert
2:00   Check lost-and-found; farewells

Getting to know you. Warm-up activities on the first day.

The Power of Unity

TO THE TEACHER

> *"Among the greatest of all services that can possibly be rendered by man to Almighty God is the education and training of children."*
> 'Abdu'l-Bahá, Selections from the Writings of 'Abdu'l-Bahá, p. 133

Teacher's Guide

The teacher's guide on the following pages contains detailed lesson plans with fun, hands-on, kid-tested learning activities. It includes copy-ready student handouts and simple patterns for making instructional materials. The lessons are user-friendly and ready-to-go with very little outside preparation needed by the teacher. They are organized in a sequential, step-by-step format, with each activity building on the previous one. Each lesson can also stand alone. The activities can be used for Bahá'í summer and winter schools, Holy Day programs, cluster gatherings and weekend retreats. They can also form part of the religious curriculum for an academic school.

This teacher's guide begins with an overview of the *Children's Classes and Retreats* series, sample schedules, an orientation program and lesson plans. These are followed by additional activities (skits, crafts, games), plans for a children's performance, student handouts, a section on music (with song sheets, musical scores and instructions for group singing), and closing activities with suggestions for follow-up. A comprehensive list of the activities in each lesson, and a separate index of activities by category (music, drama, readings, etc.), can be found at the end of the book. A compilation of selected passages on the theme of each lesson is included as a reference for teachers. A bibliography completes the manual.

Four Lessons

Each teacher's guide includes four lessons on the chosen theme. The lessons are designed to present basic Bahá'í teachings to children ages 8–12. The suggested time for each activity is in parentheses after the heading. However, if students need additional time to practice a skill, or if the class is engaged in a fruitful discussion and wishes to continue, the time can be extended, and another part of the lesson can be omitted or saved for a future class session. Be flexible.

When the lessons are used as part of an intensive program, such as a summer school or weekend retreat, you will need to select activities to fit within the time allotted. If the lessons are part of an ongoing program such as a daily or weekly academic class, one or more activities can be selected each time, until the entire course has been completed. Utilized in this way, there is sufficient material in the book for several months of weekly classes.

An ongoing class can begin with a welcome for new students, followed by singing, prayers, a review of the previous lesson (including student presentations), and the selected activities. At the beginning of each class, consider scheduling "circle time," to give children an opportunity to share news of interest to the group or to consult on pressing concerns. End the class with a review of the lesson, recitation of any memory quotes, more singing, and refreshments.

Preparing to Teach

In order to present these lessons effectively, you will need to read the lesson plan and become familiar with the objectives and the concepts to be taught. For a deeper understanding of each topic, you can also study the *References for Teachers* found at the end of this book. Your presentation should be practiced until it feels smooth and comfortable.

Explanatory notes to the teacher are not meant to be read as a script, but are intended only as a guide. Key phrases and highlights from these notes can be written on the board before or during the lesson.

All instructional materials should be made or obtained well in advance. Handouts should be photocopied for students and volunteers, and either included in their folders when they arrive, or distributed during each class as needed.

Class Discussions

During class discussions, all students should be encouraged to participate, not just the ones who speak first or loudest. A child who is silent can be asked, "Maria, what do you think about this?" Have students raise their hands rather than shouting out the answer. A simple comment like, "I'm happy to see so many of you raising your hands quietly," will reinforce this rule.

If a student's answer is incorrect, rather than saying, "No, that's wrong," it is better to respond with, "Good try. You're on the right track," or "That's an interesting thought!" Then ask another question or give a small hint that will help the child succeed. Be patient and enthusiastic. Encouragement is generally more motivating than criticism. Do not allow the children to laugh at or tease each other.

With a larger group, you may find it useful to ring a bell or develop a hand signal to bring the children back to order after a discussion or other class activity. Raising your hand while standing quietly in front of the class can be very effective. As soon as one person notices the teacher, that person should stop talking and raise his/her hand. As others notice, they should join in. Teach children the signal, and practice it a few times before starting the discussion.

Volunteers

Youth and adult volunteers can be asked to assist you with learning activities and classroom management. Volunteers can be put in charge of discussion groups. They can help with craft projects, lead the singing, teach one of the classes, work one-on-one with students who need extra assistance, and remove a disruptive child if necessary. Discipline is easier to maintain if volunteers are spaced throughout the room during the lesson.

Children's Performance*

This guidebook includes instructions for a children's performance that will give students an opportunity to demonstrate and reinforce what they have learned. Friends, families, neighbors and co-workers can be invited to the show. The fact that children will be performing in front of a live audience serves as excellent motivation for them to learn the material presented in class. The presentation may include prayers, singing, recitation of Bahá'í passages, demonstrations to illustrate various concepts, poetry, an exhibition of arts and crafts, a mini-opera and a short play.

The children's performance also provides an opportunity for home visits to parents before and after the show, to invite them and to talk in more depth about some of the themes presented.

A detailed agenda and plans for the performance are included in this manual. The children will need time to rehearse. If the program is part of a larger summer school or weekend retreat, the planning committee may schedule rehearsal time and appoint someone else to coordinate the program. During your class sessions, you might ask the performance coordinator to make note of those children who seem to grasp the material well, and who could present it in front of an audience.

> *"It is the hope of 'Abdu'l-Bahá that those youthful souls ...will be tended by one who traineth them to love."*
> 'Abdu'l-Bahá, Selections from the Writings of 'Abdu'l-Bahá, p. 134

* Note: While our student presentations have typically been scheduled for the evening, they could be held at any time. In the two-day weekend retreat format, Saturday evening is often the most convenient time for inviting neighbors and friends. This means that activities from the fourth class on Sunday morning will not be included in the presentation. If the performance follows a three-day retreat schedule or a weekly format, these activities can easily be added to the final show.

The Power of Unity

OPENING ACTIVITIES

If these lessons are being used as part of an intensive program, such as a summer school or weekend retreat, it is usually a good idea to provide some self-directed activities for children during the registration period, while they are waiting for others to arrive. After checking in, they can be shown to a table to decorate their folders or to work on other projects (see theme book #1 on *God and the Universe* for ideas). If desired, a separate table with the appropriate materials can be set up for each station. The instructions should be posted and volunteers can be asked to assist the children. These activities can also be incorporated into an ongoing weekly class.

Orientation Program

The orientation program on the first day is designed to make everyone feel welcome and to help them get to know each other. Explain to the group that we will be learning about **UNITY**, one of the most important teachings of the Bahá'í Faith, and we will focus on four main topics:

(1) The Power of Unity
(2) Unity in Diversity
(3) The Colors We Are
(4) Overcoming Prejudice

A sample orientation program is outlined below:

1. Welcome
2. Opening music
3. Selected prayers
4. Reading of the letter from the sponsoring institution
5. Introductions [A]
6. Orientation [B]
7. Review of the schedule
8. Ice-breakers and warm-up activities (see below)
9. Group singing (see song sheet in handout section)

A. <u>Introductions</u>: Each person can be asked to introduce him or herself, sharing their name, town, and one interesting personal fact. As a variation, people can be asked to act out a hobby or favorite activity, without using any words, and the group can guess what it is.

B. <u>Orientation</u>: This should cover information about classes, supervision, the role of volunteers, any house rules, food, safety, recreation and relating to others. See the *Bahá'í Children's Retreats Planning Guide* for details.

After the orientation and review of the schedule, you can organize one or two warm-up activities (see next page) which will serve as ice-breakers and help to introduce the theme. The orientation program can be followed by a snack and a short video (e.g., segments from a recent Bahá'í Newsreel), which can be played for the children during the briefing for volunteers.

The Power of Unity

Warm-up Activities

1. Unity Bingo (20-30 min.)

This is a fun mixer which has become a favorite activity at all our children's retreats. A sample Bingo sheet is included in the *Bahá'í Children's Retreats Planning Guide,* along with a blank form that can be downloaded and customized with your own set of questions (available from www. UnityWorksStore.com > click on Children's Classes).

2. Room Mixer (10-15 min.)

Ask all participants (children, youth and adults) to walk around the room, and as you call out each item below, they should gather with others who have the same characteristic, then introduce themselves.

For example, for the first item, everyone with very short hair will be in one group. People with shoulder-length hair will be in another, and those with long hair will be in a third group. If someone doesn't have an exact match, they should come as close as they can. Give them a minute or two to introduce themselves before calling out the next item. You can vary the list to fit the participants.

    a. The same length hair   c. The same type of shoes   e. The same birth month
    b. The same color shirt   d. The same height   f . (your item here)

3. Group Match (10-15 min.)

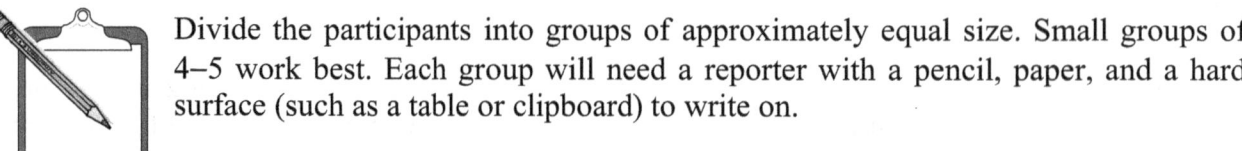

Divide the participants into groups of approximately equal size. Small groups of 4–5 work best. Each group will need a reporter with a pencil, paper, and a hard surface (such as a table or clipboard) to write on.

Tell the class to think of the things they have in common with <u>all</u> the other members of their group. <u>Every</u> member must have it. But there's a catch: it can't be anything visible that we can see in this room. For example, everyone in the group might have a nose—but we can see that! They will have to look deeper. Perhaps everyone in the group has a pet, or has traveled to another country, or speaks Spanish, or likes carrots, or has finished first grade. You get the idea.

Give the groups about five minutes to work, and offer small prizes to the team with the longest list. Of course, they will have to read their list out loud before receiving their reward.

The Power of Unity

4. Venn Diagram (5-10 min.)

Ask participants to pair up with someone they don't yet know well, and to make a Venn diagram of some of their favorite things. (Draw an example on the board.)

Section A will include things only Person "A" likes. Section B will include things only Person "B" likes. Section C, where the circles overlap, will include things they both like (see below).

Each pair will need a blank diagram (on following page) and something to write with. Give them about five minutes to work. When finished, ask for a few volunteers to share.

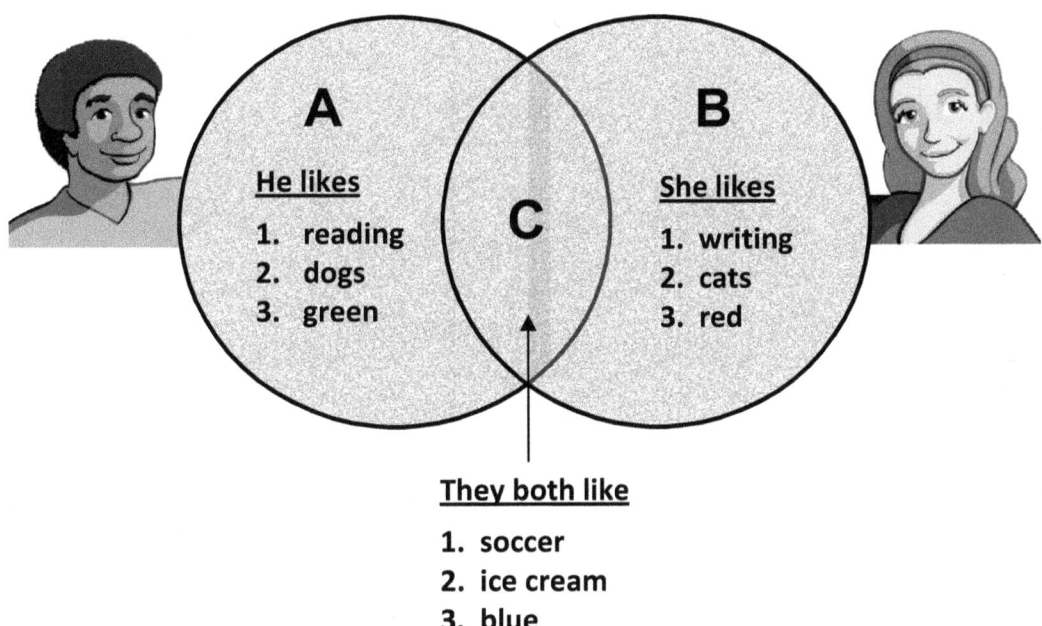

Note to teachers: A *Venn Diagram* is made up of two or more overlapping circles. It is used to show relationships between sets—or different groups of things. Here, we are using it to explore similarities and differences between two people. The Venn diagram was developed in 1880 by English mathematician John Venn.

The Power of Unity

Venn Diagram: Work with your partner to make a list of some of your favorite things. List things that only one person likes in the left outer circle, and things only the other person likes in the right outer circle. List things that you both like in the middle section where the circles overlap.

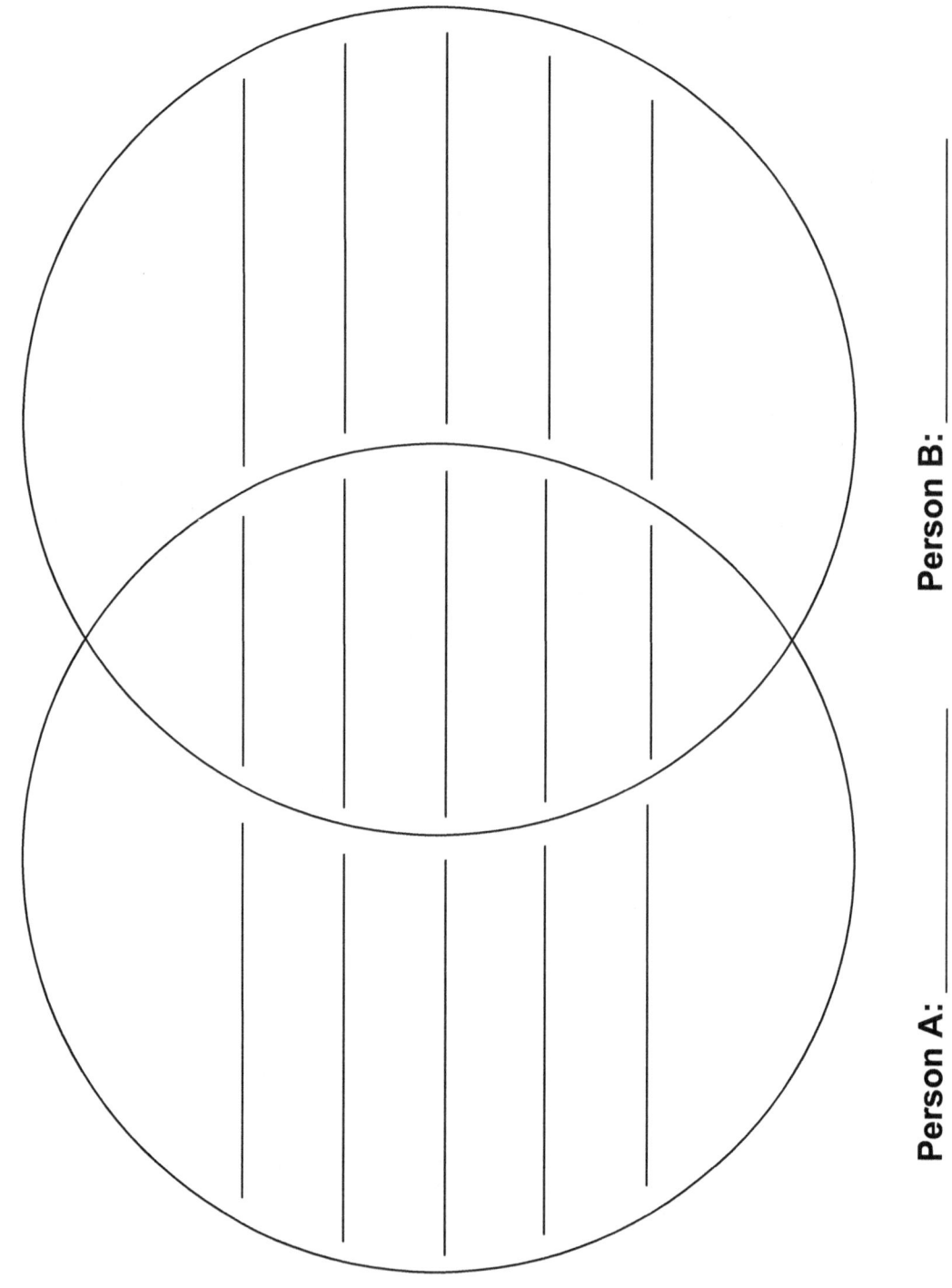

Person A: _____

Person B: _____

5. Getting to Know You Chart (10-15 min.)

As a variation on the same theme, you can divide the participants into small groups of 4–5 people, and ask each group to fill in a "Getting to Know You" chart (see sample below). There will be some similarities and many differences as well. The group charts can then be posted on the wall, giving people an opportunity to learn more about the rest of their classmates. The categories in the left column can be modified to fit the participants. If a digital camera and printer are available, a photo of each person can be added to the chart.

Sample Chart

"Getting to Know You"

NAME	Jesse	Carmel			
Photo					
Age	10	8			
Special talent	drawing	gymnastics			
Favorite subject	science	math			
Favorite place	ocean	my room			
Favorite song	Silent Night	Raindrops			
Favorite color	blue	blue			
Favorite food	tacos	peanut butter			
Favorite animal	Buddy (my dog)	horses			
Favorite game	tennis	chess			

The Power of Unity

"Getting to Know You"

NAME						
Photo						
Age						
Special talent						
Favorite subject						
Favorite place						
Favorite song						
Favorite color						
Favorite food						
Favorite animal						
Favorite game						

Copy this page to make one chart for each group.

Bahá'í Children's Classes and Retreats: Theme 5, p. 18

The Power of Unity

Additional Opening Activities

Videos

During the volunteer orientation (see *Bahá'í Children's Retreats Planning Guide* for details), the children may wish to watch excerpts from one of the following videos, which are related to the theme of unity.

The Power of Race Unity: This documentary was produced in 1998 by the National Spiritual Assembly of the Bahá'ís of the United States. Of particular interest is the segment which profiles Anisa Kintz, who at the age of eight, founded the *Calling All Colors Conference*, a kids' program to combat racism and prejudice. This is a forceful example of what a single child can do to advance the cause of unity. The video is currently available for viewing online:

> http://bahai-videos.com. Type "power race unity" (no quotes) in the search box on the top right. Scroll down to the bottom of the page and click on the video title. Turn up the sound and click play.

Starting Small: Teaching Children Tolerance: This 1997 video by Margie McGovern, profiles seven exemplary classrooms in which teachers are helping children learn about tolerance and respect. Of particular relevance is the first segment, which shows elementary school children finding out about their own skin colors and painting multicultural face pictures. The video comes with a teacher's guide and is free to schools, home school networks, religious groups and non-profit organizations working with children or youth. Free orders must be authorized by the organization's director.

> Write to: Teaching Tolerance Order Department, 400 Washington Avenue, Montgomery, AL 36104 USA. Allow eight weeks for delivery. Order forms can be downloaded from: http://www.tolerance.org/kit/starting-small. The video is also available from: www.Amazon.com.

Jigsaw Puzzles

As an alternative to the videos, a few jigsaw puzzles of various levels of difficulty can be set out for the children to work on. Puzzles can be enjoyed by all ages. Puzzles provide an opportunity for teamwork and collaborative problem solving, and they are inexpensive and fun.

Evening Snack

S'mores (mini marshmallows and chocolate bits, sandwiched between graham crackers and microwaved for about 30 seconds) make a great "multicultural" snack for the unity retreat. The marshmallows can also be toasted on sticks over a campfire.

The Power of Unity

"The education and training of children is among the most meritorious acts of humankind."
- 'Abdu'l-Bahá, Selections from the Writings of 'Abdu'l-Bahá, p. 129

LESSON #1

The Power of Unity

The Power of Unity – Lesson #1

The Power of Unity

Objectives: Students will be able to:
- Identify unity as one of the most important teachings of Bahá'u'lláh.
- Define unity and disunity, and give examples of each.
- List some of the benefits of unity.
- Explain that people are different, but there is only one human race, and God wants us to be united.

Before class, prepare all instructional materials on the list at the end of this lesson. Post pictures of people and arrange the flowers. Write the memory quote neatly on the board with one phrase on each line. Orient volunteer assistants. Distribute folders and pens to all.

---

1. SONG: "God Is One" (5 min.)

Have students take out their song sheets and sing along. Ask the music coordinator for assistance if needed.

2. INTRODUCTION (2 min.)

Ask students:

- Do you remember how God speaks to humankind? *(Through His Messengers.)*
- That's right! Do you remember some of their names? *(Moses, Jesus, etc.)*
- Good. And Who is the Messenger of God for today? *(Bahá'u'lláh.)*
- Today, we will learn about one of Bahá'u'lláh's <u>most important</u> teachings: **UNITY**.
- Bahá'u'lláh says: *"So powerful is the light of unity that it can illuminate the whole earth."*
- That's pretty important! So let's find out what "unity" means.

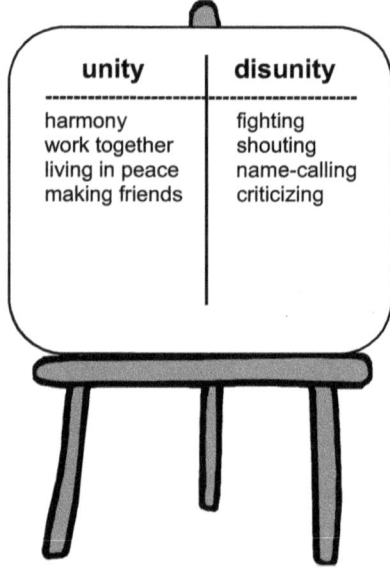

3. DEFINITIONS (5 min.)

Using large print, write the words **unity** and **disunity** in two columns at the top of a second whiteboard or poster. Have students write these same words at the top of the notebook paper in their folders. Ask them to find a partner and quickly brainstorm examples or definitions for each word.

Give students a minute to work, then have them share their lists. Take one suggestion from each person so everyone has a chance to participate, and make brief notes on the board.

Bahá'í Children's Classes and Retreats: Theme 5, p. 22

The Power of Unity – Lesson #1

4. READING: "Unity is / Disunity is" (5-10 min.)

Have students take out the stapled packet on *The Power of Unity* (see handouts section of this book) and turn to the third page (also included at the end of this lesson for convenience). Ask for youth or adult volunteers to read the items in the first box (Unity is…), and the second box (Disunity is…). Choose people with expressive voices who read well.

Then ask the class:

- How do we feel when we are unified?
  (happy, friendly, peaceful…)

- How do we feel when we are disunified?
  (angry, sad, frustrated…)

- Do you think the world is unified now?
  (accept all opinions)

Have the children raise their hands to answer.

5. PANTOMIME (5-10 min.)

Explain to the students that they are going to demonstrate what unity and disunity look like, using movements, but no words. If you have a small class, divide them in half. Tell the first group, they will illustrate **disunity**. The second group will illustrate **unity**. For a large class, select six students, and form two groups with three students each. The rest will be observers.

Give them about ten seconds to plan. (No offensive gestures, please.) Then ask the two groups to share their dramatizations, one at a time. When finished, ask the class: *Which group would you rather join? What kind of world would you rather live in?* Allow time for a brief discussion if the students are interested.

6. THE BENEFITS OF UNITY (up to 45 min.)

Depending on the time available, select one or more of the following activities to demonstrate some of the benefits of diversity. After each activity, ask the class what they learned.

A. <u>Sticks</u>: Give one child a thin stick to break. (This should be easy.) Then give the child a lot of thin sticks tied together in a bundle. (This should be impossible to break.) What can be learned from this? *(There is strength in unity.)*

The Power of Unity – Lesson #1

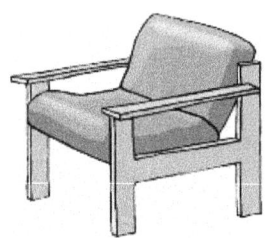

B. <u>Chair</u>: Have one child sit in a sturdy chair at the front of the room. Four other children enter and, one by one, each tries to lift the chair without success. (They can flex their muscles, struggle, grunt, wipe the sweat from their brow, look discouraged—really hamming it up, to show how difficult it is.)

After each child has tried it alone, have them huddle together and quietly consult on a solution. Then have them stand at the sides and back of the chair. One child can say aloud "1, 2 3!" and together they lift the chair and its occupant, carry it a few steps, then gently set it down. What can be learned? *(We can do it together!)*

C. <u>Donkey Tug o' War</u>: Select two children of similar size and strength to be hungry donkeys. Tie them together with one end of the rope around each donkey's waist. Place two "food bowls" at opposite ends of the room.

Tell the class that the donkeys are very hungry and each wants to eat from its own bowl, but they may not remove the rope. (Quietly remind the donkeys that they are only acting, and shouldn't be too forceful.) Divide the class in half and tell each half to cheer for a different donkey. Give the signal, and let the donkey's pull against each other, each trying to get to its own bowl without success.

Let them struggle for a few moments, then stop the action and ask them to consult. How can they both eat without removing the rope? *(They will need to take turns.)* Ask the class what was learned. *(Problems can be solved by consulting and cooperating.)*

Make sure there is sufficient space for this activity, a thick rope or tie that won't cut at the waist, and a bell to stop the action if necessary.

Drawing courtesy of Phil Bartle, Ph.D.
www.scn.org/cmp/ex-illu.htm - #13

D. <u>Hot and Cold</u>: Show the class a small object, then ask for a student volunteer to leave the room. Hide the object. Then invite the volunteer to return and search for it, while the rest of the class says "warm, warmer, hot…" or "cold, colder, freezing…" as the student gets closer or farther away from it.

Once the object has been found, ask what can be learned from this demonstration. *(The importance of cooperation; working together we can achieve our goal.)*

Note: The children often ask to repeat this demonstration with additional volunteers.

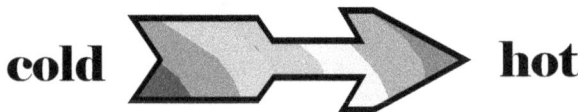

The Power of Unity – Lesson #1

E. <u>Shoe Demonstration</u>: As a demonstration of human interdependence, call on one of the children to hold up his or her shoe. Choose someone with a shoe made up of at least three materials (rubber, canvas, leather, plastic, metal, cotton, velcro, etc.), and have a suitable backup shoe with you just in case.

* Idea suggested by Steven Gottlieb

- Ask the class what the shoe is made of, and list the materials on the board.
- Then mention the first item (e.g., rubber), and ask where it comes from. *(Rubber trees.)*
- Where do rubber trees grow? *(In the Amazon jungle, Southeast Asian rainforest, etc.)*
- How do we get the rubber from the trees? *(A cut is made in the tree bark, which allows the "latex" to flow out into a bucket. It is then collected and processed.)*

> **See the following websites for a brief description with photos:**
> * www.kepu.ac.cn/english/banna/tropic/tro418_01.html
> * www.bio.ilstu.edu/armstrong/syllabi/rubber/rubber.htm

- Who made the rubber harvesting tools and what are they made from?
- How does rubber get from the tree to the shoe factory?
- Who drives the trucks? What are trucks made of?
- Who designed and built the trucks? Where do we get fuel for the trucks?
- Who made the roads for the trucks to drive on? What are roads made of?

Continue with this type of questioning for each material composing the shoe—or at least until the children understand the point: that we depend on many other people for even the simplest of things. Ask how many individuals they think might be involved in the making of one shoe and bringing it to market. *(Thousands)*

<u>Ask</u>: What can we learn from this? *(The importance of cooperation; we depend on others and they depend on us; our complex modern society requires a diversity of knowledge and skills, which requires a division of labor; we need each other.)*

The Power of Unity – Lesson #1

F. <u>Word Puzzle</u>: Give each student a copy of the word puzzle (in the handouts section of this book) and ask them to determine the common word or phrase illustrated in each box. Do the first one with them so they understand the task (see puzzle with answers below). Then give them one minute to finish the entire page, each working alone. No talking!

Give them one more minute working in pairs; and another minute in groups of four if necessary. Then review the entire page with the whole class. Usually, as more people work together, more answers are found. What was learned? *(The value of diverse opinions; some problems are easier to solve in groups; two heads are better than one.)*

sandbox	man overboard	I understand	pair of dice (or) paradise
1 SAND	2 I MAN BOARD	3 STAND I	4 DICE DICE
5 WEAR LONG	6 R O ROADS D S	7 RIGHT TIME	8 CYCLE CYCLE CYCLE
long underwear	crossroads	right on time	tricycle (or) recycle

G. <u>Summary</u>: Ask students to pair up with the nearest classmate and share what they have learned about the benefits of unity. Give them a minute to consult, then call on volunteers to share one of their insights. Write their answers on the board.

7. READING: *"Unity"* (15-20 min.)

Ask students to take out their packets and turn to the fifth page on "Unity." (The teacher's version with embedded questions and comments, is found at the end of this lesson.) Read the quote and first paragraph out loud, then ask:

- How many races of people are there in the world?
  (That's right! Only one.)

- What is it called?
  (The human race.)

Have children raise their hands to answer.

Then ask selected children or youth volunteers to read each remaining paragraph out loud, make up a question or two about it, and call on other children to answer—just as you did. If necessary, encourage them to call on someone who hasn't yet had a chance. If you call on some of the more capable children first, the others will more readily understand how this method of student questioning works.

The Power of Unity – Lesson #1

8. MEMORY QUOTE: "So powerful…" (5-10 min.)

Have students take out their page of quotations and locate quote #1: "So powerful is the light of unity…" (The quote should already be written on the board.)

A. **Understanding:** Read the quote aloud slowly, then ask students:

- Who said these words? *(Bahá'u'lláh)*
- What does "illuminate" mean? *(To light up)*
- What is Bahá'u'lláh telling us?
  (Unity is like a bright light in the darkness. It has the power to bring peace and progress to the world.)

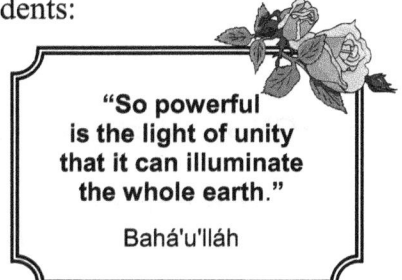

"So powerful is the light of unity that it can illuminate the whole earth."
Bahá'u'lláh

B. **Repetition:** Read the quote again slowly and have students repeat after each phrase. Read it again, faster. Then read two phrases at a time as students repeat. (You can use gestures as a memory aid. Flex your arm muscle when saying the word *"powerful,"* clasp your hands together when saying *"unity,"* spread your fingers wide for *"illuminate,"* and move your hand in a wide arc for *"the whole earth."*)

C. **Backwards Buildup:** Read the last phrase and have students repeat until it is memorized. Then add the previous phrase and read through to the end. Continue in this manner until you have reached the beginning. By that time, most children will have the entire passage memorized.

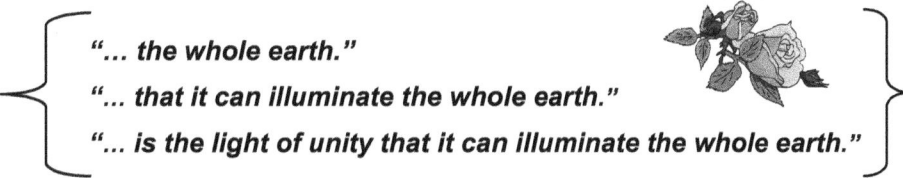

"… the whole earth."
"… that it can illuminate the whole earth."
"… is the light of unity that it can illuminate the whole earth."

D. **Disappearing Act:** Then, using an eraser, swipe a narrow diagonal path through the entire passage on the board. This will leave a blank space on each line. Ask for student volunteers to read the passage again. Let everyone take a turn. Then make another eraser swipe and ask for another round of volunteers. Continue until the passage has completely disappeared.

E. **Recitation:** Ask for student volunteers to recite the whole quote from memory. Call on the most capable ones first so they can serve as models.

> *Tell students they can work with a friend and use these techniques to memorize other quotes for the children's performance. Encourage them to memorize additional passages after returning home.*

The Power of Unity – Lesson #1

9. CLOSING QUESTIONS (1 min.)

Ask the students:

- What is one of the most important teachings of Bahá'u'lláh? *(Unity.)*
- Why does God want us to be united? *(For our own happiness, and for the peace, progress and security of the world.)*

10. SONG: "Si Estamos Juntos" (4 min.)

Have students take out their song sheets and sing along. Ask the music coordinator for assistance if needed.

Collect all folders and pencils.

11. CRAFT: Lanyards (30-45 min.)

Craft activities are designed to reinforce the material presented during class. A braided lanyard is a concrete example of the strength that comes from unity. Children can make a variety of lanyard projects including key chains, bike streamers, shoe bobs, bracelets, barrettes and zipper pulls. See page 50 for instructions and ideas.

After the lesson, dismiss the children for a break before Class #2.

Demonstrating unity – Activity #5

The Power of Unity – Lesson #1

Unity Is:

- Knowing that humankind is one family
- Treating all people with respect
- Valuing diversity
- Serving others
- Consulting together
- Making sure everyone is included
- Listening and trying to understand
- Working to make things better for all
- Solving conflicts peacefully
- Loving others, even when they aren't perfect
- Showing cooperation and teamwork
- Forgiving people
- Making friends

Disunity Is:

- Being selfish
- Insisting on your own way
- Not getting along with others
- Thinking you are better than everyone else
- Showing prejudice and hatred
- Shouting at people
- Telling lies about others
- Leaving people out
- Name calling and putdowns
- Laughing when someone makes a mistake
- Arguing or fighting
- Hurting other people
- Not caring about others
- Backbiting

The Power of Unity – Lesson #1

Teacher's Version

 UNITY

"The earth is but one country, and mankind its citizens."
(Bahá'u'lláh, Gleanings, p. 250)

One Human Family: There is only one race of people in the world. Do you know what it is called? That's right! It's the human race, and we all belong to it. We come in different shapes, sizes and colors, but we are one human family, children of one God.

We may be young or old, short or tall, male or female. We may have dark skin, light skin, or a color in-between. Some of us were born in China, South Africa, India or Brazil. We may speak English, Spanish, Arabic or Japanese. Some of us are good at sports, others at math, music or art. Some are Christians, Jews, Hindus, Muslims or Bahá'ís. We are diverse in many ways, but we live on one planet. One God created us all.

> **Ask:** Do you know how many countries there are in the world? *(Almost 200)*
> * How many languages? *(Over 5,000)*
> * How many races? *(One. Scientists tested blood samples from people all around the world, and they discovered that we are all related!)*

The Importance of Unity: Bahá'u'lláh tells us that God wants His children to live in unity. We should treat each other with justice and love. He said the whole human race was created from the same dust, so no one should look down on anyone else. Bahá'u'lláh says that countries must stop fighting wars and all people must work together for peace. But we won't have peace, until we first have unity. We must be united with our brothers and sisters all around the world.

> Show globe or photo of the earth from space, and pictures of people from around the world.

"The well-being of mankind, its peace and security, are unattainable unless and until its unity is firmly established."
(Bahá'u'lláh, Gleanings, p. 286)

We Are Connected: People who understand unity know that everything in the whole universe is connected. Everything depends on something else to live. Animals must eat other animals or plants in order to survive. Plants need sunshine and rain to grow. Human beings are also connected to each other like links in a chain. Everything we do affects our planet and the other people on it.
Every link is important. You are one of the links in that chain.

The Power of Unity: Unity is a powerful force that can connect us all. It can connect our families, communities and nations. Unity gives us strength. We are more powerful working together than alone. Unity is like medicine for the world's sickness. Unity will bring peace, progress and light to the world.

"So powerful is the light of unity that it can illuminate the whole earth."
(Bahá'u'lláh, Gleanings, p. 288)

Bahá'í Children's Classes and Retreats: Theme 5, p. 30

The Power of Unity – Lesson #1

MATERIALS NEEDED

- White board, easel, markers, eraser
- Second white board or some poster board or chart paper
- Folder, notebook paper, pen or pencil for each student
- Dictionary
- Large world map or globe
- Song sheets and page of quotations for each student [A]
- Packet of readings on "The Power of Unity" [A]
- Teacher's version of the handout titled "Unity" (included with this lesson)
- Pictures of diverse people from around the world [B]
- Flowers [C]
- Skit materials:
  - A thin stick, plus about 50 more sticks tied in a bundle [D]
  - A sturdy moveable chair
  - Two food bowls and a bell for the donkey activity
  - A rope or long strip of cloth (approx. 5 yards or 5 meters) to tie the "donkeys"
  - A small object to hide for the "hot and cold" skit
  - Backup shoe for the interdependence demonstration
  - Copies of the word puzzle for each student (in Handouts section) (Photocopy and cut along the dotted line to make two per page.)
  - Answers to the word puzzle [E]
- Photo of the Earth from space [F]
- References for teachers (included at the end of this manual)

A. Included in the Handouts section of this manual. The student handouts, along with full-page color illustrations to accompany the lessons, are available in the download packet for this teacher's guide: **www.UnityWorksStore.com** > Children's Classes > The Power of Unity > student handouts. The illustrations can be posted on the wall during classes as an aide for visual learners and to help bring the lessons and readings to life.

B. Photographs of people can be found in Bahá'í booklets on race unity, in the Bahá'í Media Bank online (http://media.bahai.org/subjects/activities), in National Geographic Magazine (www.nationalgeographic.com), at teacher supply stores in the social studies section, from educational textbook publishers under classroom posters, and clip art. We have also included a selection of faces in the download packet for this teacher's guide, available from: **www.UnityWorksStore.com.** The images can be laminated and posted around the room.

C. Real or artificial flowers can be arranged around the classroom or taped next to the photographs of people to embellish them. Large, vivid pictures of flowers can also be found in gardening magazines and seed catalogs, available from many hardware stores and online.

D. Wooden skewers from the grocery store meat department are inexpensive and perfectly suited for this activity. Cut off the sharp points before giving them to the children.

E. Answers to word puzzle:

> 1. sandbox
> 2. man overboard
> 3. I understand
> 4. paradise or pair of dice
> 5. long underwear
> 6. crossroads
> 7. right on time
> 8. tricycle or recycle

F. This image is in the public domain and may be used freely with acknowledgment to NASA.

Download and print it from:

<http://nssdc.gsfc.nasa.gov/image/planetary/earth/apollo17_earth.jpg>.

Posters and prints are also available for sale through teacher supply stores, science museums, and by emailing NASA at: request@mail630.gsfc.nasa.gov or by calling (301) 286-6695.

* * * * *

LESSON #2

Unity in Diversity

The Power of Unity – Lesson #2

Unity in Diversity

Objectives: Students will be able to:
- List some similarities and differences among human beings.
- Explain why diversity is important.
- Distinguish between unity and sameness.
- Describe the concept of unity in diversity using concrete examples.

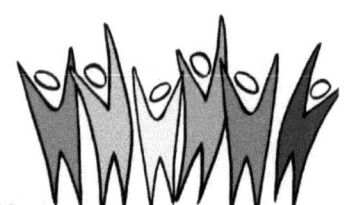

Before class, prepare all instructional materials on the list at the end of this lesson. Set up craft activity centers. Orient assistants for discussions and craft projects. Make space for activity #2. Set up felt board. Distribute folders and pencils to each student.

---

1. **MEMORY QUOTE: "So powerful…"** (2-3 min.)

   Ask for a few volunteers to recite from memory the quote learned during lesson one: *"So powerful is the light of unity that it can illuminate the whole earth."*

2. **SIMILARITIES AND DIFFERENCES** (15-20 min.)

   Ask the class:

   - What is one of the most important teachings of Bahá'u'lláh? *(That's right. Unity! But unity doesn't mean sameness.)*

   - Look around at the people in this room. Are we all exactly the same? *(We're alike in some ways and different in others.)*

   - Let's look at some of the similarities. How many things can you name that ALL humans have in common? *(Obviously barring an accident or medical condition.)*

   Write their answers on the board.

   > a. Physical characteristics? *(bellybutton, arms, legs, eyes, skin…)*
   > b. Feelings? *(sadness, joy, anger, fear, hope…)*
   > c. Physical needs (not wants)? *(air, water, food, shelter, clothing, sleep…)*
   > d. Spiritual or emotional needs? *(faith, love, justice, family, friends…)*
   > e. Other commonalities? *(all created by God, all live on the same earth, breathe the same air, all have parents, talents, a body, a soul…)*

   - Look around again. What are some of the differences? *(We all have noses, but they are different shapes. We all need to eat, but we like different foods….)*

Bahá'í Children's Classes and Retreats: Theme 5, p. 34

The Power of Unity – Lesson #2

- Let's look at some other similarities and differences:

Have all the children stand up in a tight group in the center of the room. Ask them to move left (all the way to one side of the room) if they are the oldest child in their family, or to move right (all the way to the other side) if they are not the oldest. (Adopted children can consider their biological or adoptive family.) Continue down the list.

Have children move to the left or right as you call out each characteristic below:

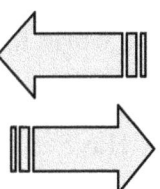

- oldest child in family
- born in Our Town
- speak more than one language
- under the age of ten
- can do a cartwheel
- have pierced ears
- like pizza
- have a pet
- can multiply 12 x 12
- have been to a Pow Wow
- like to do art
- like to sing or dance
- like to play sports
- are girls
- are boys
- belong to the human race

If there is not enough room to move back and forth, you can take the children outside or have them stand up and sit down instead. You can also create your own list to suit the children in your group.

When finished, have the children return to their seats and ask what we can learn from this demonstration. *(We are alike and different in many ways.)* Let children know that it's okay to be different. No one else in the world is exactly like you!

3. LEAVES OF ONE TREE (5 min.)

Show the class a tree branch, or even better a live tree, and ask:

- Are all the leaves on this branch exactly the same?
  (No. They are similar but have different colors, shapes and sizes.)
- What do all the leaves share in common? *(All leaves; all attached to the same branch.)*
- What happens to a leaf that is separated from the branch—like this? *(It dies.)*
- Bahá'u'lláh says that people are like the leaves of one branch, the fruits of one tree, and the flowers of one garden. *(As you speak, hold up a basket filled with fruit and a vase with diverse flowers.)* What do you think He means?

4. READING: "Unity in Diversity" (10-15 min.)

Have students take out their packet of readings and turn to the page titled *"Unity in Diversity."* (A copy is included at the end of this lesson for convenience.) Read the title and the quote. Then call on capable volunteers to read each paragraph out loud, except for the bulleted list of questions in the middle section. This list should be read by the teacher and answered by the class. Have each reader make up one or two questions about that paragraph and call on other children to answer. Encourage them to call on someone who hasn't yet had a chance. Have the children raise their hands.

The Power of Unity – Lesson #2

5. MUSICAL DEMONSTRATION (5 min.)

A. Hum a single musical note and ask the class to hum it with you. *(Hmmm......)* Then sing *"Row, row, row your boat"* (or other common song) with the children, but tell them they can only use that one note. The song will sound rather dull. Explain that this is a demonstration of **sameness**. Bo-ring!

B. Next, tell the children that when you give the signal, they should loudly make as many different noises as they can. You should hear squawking, hooting, hissing, howling, barking and other discordant sounds. Stop the children after a few seconds, and explain that this demonstrates **diversity without unity**. It's what we have in the world today.

C. Then quickly divide the class into three groups (approximately equal in size), and give each group one note of a chord. The music leader can help with this. Have each group hum its note separately, then have all sing together for (hopefully) a pleasing sound. Explain that this is a demonstration of **unity in diversity**, and it takes lots of practice.

6. FELT LESSON: "The Eye" (5-10 min.)

Present the felt lesson on "The Eye" (see patterns and instructions at the end of this lesson). If there is time, ask several children if they would like to try it in front of the class without your help. They may also wish to volunteer for the children's performance.

7. MACHINES IN MOTION (15-20 min.)

Divide the children into small groups of 3-4, and give each group a different machine to act out. They can use movements and sound effects, but no words. Each child will be one part of the whole machine. The examples on the following page will give you some ideas, but it is better to use your own examples with machines appropriate to the local culture and level of technology. Allow children to pick something else if the item they are given seems too difficult.

Groups should keep their item a secret. Ask them to think about what kinds of sounds it makes. How do the different parts move? How does each part work together? Give the groups a few minutes to practice in private, checking on them to be sure the instructions are understood.

When ready, bring the groups together to perform their pantomimes, while the class tries to guess what each item is. When finished, ask the class how these examples illustrate the principle of unity in diversity. *(Each part plays a critical role in the functioning of the machine. It also has to work in harmony with all the other parts, in order to get the job done.)*

> As a follow-up activity, some children may wish to visit this website for a description of basic machines: www.mos.org/sln/leonardo/inventorstoolbox.html

Bahá'í Children's Classes and Retreats: Theme 5, p. 36

The Power of Unity – Lesson #2

Machines in Motion: *This page can be photocopied, and the cards cut out and distributed, one to each group for activity #7. The images will help children visualize the functions of each machine. The cards can be laminated for greater durability if you plan to re-use them.*

airplane	bicycle	blender	clock
lawn mower	photo-copier	bow and arrow	audio player
tractor	toaster	television	robot
sewing machine	vacuum cleaner	vending machine	washing machine

Bahá'í Children's Classes and Retreats: Theme 5, p. 37

The Power of Unity – Lesson #2

8. DISCUSSION: "Unity in Diversity" (20-30 min.)

Divide the class into the same small groups and assign a youth or adult volunteer to lead each group. If there aren't enough volunteers, you can form larger groups.

Give every volunteer a copy of "Unity in Diversity: Discussion Questions" (included at the end of this lesson). As group facilitators, they should ask the questions, and encourage the children to share their thoughts. Groups can move to another room or outside if desired.

Allow about 15 minutes for them to work. Walk around to observe the discussions. Then bring the children back together to share their thoughts. Ask each group to contribute one insight from their discussion. Write these on the board. Go around again until all the ideas have been shared.

9. MEMORY QUOTE: "Regard ye not..." (5-10 min.)

For a weekend retreat, you might have children only memorize one quote ("So powerful..." from lesson #1). For an ongoing class, they could memorize a different quote each time.

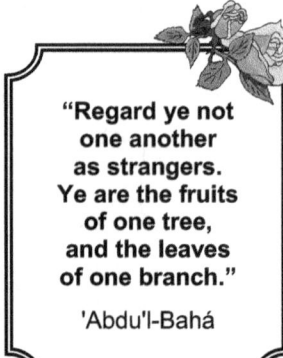

"Regard ye not one another as strangers. Ye are the fruits of one tree, and the leaves of one branch."
'Abdu'l-Bahá

Have students take out their quotations page and locate quote #8: *"Regard y not one another as strangers…"*

Write the quote on the board, with one phrase on each line. Read the quote aloud slowly, then ask students:

- Who said these words? *('Abdu'l-Bahá)*
- What does "stranger" mean? *(An unknown person)*
- What is 'Abdu'l-Bahá telling us? *(Don't see each other as outsiders. You are all like leaves growing on the same tree of humanity.)*

As appropriate, explain that there are some "bad strangers" who children should not befriend.

Continue with the memorization process outlined in Lesson #1 (p. 27).

You can use gestures and objects as memory aids. For example, push your hand out (with palm open and elbow straight) as if pushing someone away, when saying *"strangers."* Hold up a fruit when saying "fruits of one tree," and a leaf when saying "leaves of one branch."

The Power of Unity – Lesson #2

10. SONG: "One Planet, One People" (5-10 min.)

Have students take out their song sheets and sing along. Ask the music coordinator for assistance if needed.

Collect all folders and pencils.

11. CRAFT ACTIVITIES (30-60 min.)

Craft activities are designed to reinforce material presented during the class. Instructions for each craft project are included at the end of this lesson.

After this activity, dismiss the children for lunch and quiet time.

* * * * *

UNITY IN DIVERSITY

"Be as one spirit, one soul, leaves of one tree, flowers of one garden…"

('Abdu'l-Bahá, Promulgation of Universal Peace, p. 24)

Imagine the flowers in a garden. 'Abdu'l-Bahá says that each flower has a different shape, its own special color and sweet-smelling perfume. But they all grow from the same earth, the same sun shines upon them, and the same clouds give them rain. Each flower is pleasing by itself, but when the different flowers are all together, the garden is even more beautiful.

It is the same with people. We are like beautiful flowers growing in a garden. We each have a different shape and our own special color. We speak different languages, wear different clothing, and enjoy different music and food. But we all live upon the same earth, breathe the same air, and are children of the same heavenly Father. Our diversity adds beauty to garden of humanity.

The Value of Diversity

- Think of all the colors in nature. Can you name some of them?
- Can you imagine if the entire world were all <u>one</u> color? Which color should it be?
- Would a rainbow be as beautiful if all the bands were the same shade?
- Could you bake a cake with only one ingredient?
- What if all the musical instruments in an orchestra made the same sound?

Just think how dull it would be if all people everywhere looked and acted and thought and talked and dressed exactly the same! What if you had to eat the same food every day, wear the same clothes, read the same books and think the same thoughts, for the rest of your life? What if you never, <u>ever</u> got to try anything new? And what if all your friends were exactly like you?

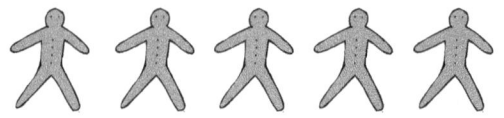

Diversity is important because it gives us beauty, variety, choices and new ideas.

Unity is Not Sameness

Unity does not mean sameness. Unity means respecting our differences and working together in harmony. It means knowing that each part has something valuable to contribute to the whole. Each member of the human family has something special to offer to the human race.

When we have **unity in diversity**, there is harmony, like the sound of different notes joined together in a perfect chord. We are showing unity in diversity, when we all work and play and live together in peace.

The Power of Unity – Lesson #2

"The Eye"

Teacher's Guide, Script, and Patterns for Felt Lesson

TO THE TEACHER: This packet contains instructions, a script, and patterns for making a felt lesson on "The Eye: An Example of Unity in Diversity." In order to present the lesson, you will need either a felt board or carpet board (see instructions on following pages). A carpet board is more durable and has a more finished look. After preparing the board and cutting out the pattern pieces, read through the script and repeat the actions until you can present the lesson smoothly. The objectives of the lesson are listed below. The children will be able to:

| (1) Depict the eye as a concrete example of unity in diversity. | (2) Give specific examples of why diversity is important. | (3) Explain the difference between unity and sameness. |

The Power of Unity – Lesson #2

Script for Felt Lesson

"The Eye"

	NARRATION	ACTION	
1	The eye is an example of unity in diversity.	Place large white eye in center of felt board.	
2	Each part of the eye has a different job, but they all work together for the same goal.	Place blue circle in center of eye; then add black circle on top.	
3	For example, the pupil is the black opening in front of the eye that admits light so we can see.	Point to black pupil.	
4	The iris opens and closes, changing the size of the pupil to let in just the right amount of light.	Point to blue iris.	
5	What would happen if all the parts of the eye were the same?	Place white circle over other circles.	

Questions for the class

1. What are the different parts of the eye?
2. What is the function of each part?
3. What would happen if one part didn't work or didn't want to cooperate with the others?
4. What can we learn about unity in diversity from this example?

The parts of the eye are different, but they all work together, and all are necessary for sight.

Bahá'í Children's Classes and Retreats: Theme 5, p. 42

The Power of Unity – Lesson #2

Instructions for Making Felt or Carpet Board

A felt board can be purchased at a teacher supply store, or one can be constructed by gluing a large piece of felt onto a stiff backing such as heavy cardboard, thin plywood or masonite. Spray glue gives the best results. A carpet board is constructed in the same way. Felt and glue are available at yardage and craft supply stores.

Materials

- Sharp scissors
- Large piece of felt or indoor-outdoor carpet*
  (choose beige or other neutral color,
  approx. 24 x 36 in. or 60 x 90 cm.)
- Backing board (same size as felt or carpet)
- Spray glue or white craft glue

  * If using carpet, test a piece of felt to be sure it sticks.
  Some types of carpeting may work better than others.

Instructions for Making Felt Pieces

1. Photocopy the pattern pages.
2. Using the copies, cut around each shape outside the line.
3. Use tape or large paper clips to attach each pattern to the correct color of felt.
4. Carefully cut out each felt piece, using the pattern as a guide.
5. Store the script and felt pieces in a zip-lock plastic bag for ease of use.

Materials

- Pattern pieces (on following pages)
- Sharp scissors
- Pieces of black, white and light blue felt
- Double-stick or regular tape

The Power of Unity - Lesson #2

Pattern for felt lesson on "The Eye"

Cut from white felt.

Patterns can be enlarged on a photocopier if desired.

Tip: For easier cut-outs, photocopy patterns onto peel-and-stick adhesive paper.

Bahá'í Children's Classes and Retreats: Theme 5, p. 44

The Power of Unity – Lesson #2

Patterns for Felt Lesson on "The Eye"

Bahá'í Children's Classes and Retreats: Theme 5, p. 45

The Power of Unity – Lesson #2

UNITY IN DIVERSITY
Discussion Questions

Instructions for group facilitator: Gather your small group and find a quiet place to work. Your job is to ask the questions below, and encourage all of the children to share their thoughts. A child who is silent can be asked, "What do you think about this?" Do not allow the children to laugh at or tease each other. Take notes below, and prepare the children to share their answers. You will have about 15 minutes for this activity.

1. What does unity in diversity mean?

2. What is the difference between unity and sameness?

3. Why is diversity important?

4. Is it possible to fight with someone and still be unified?
   (No. Fighting is an example of disunity.)

5. Is it possible to disagree with someone and still be unified?
   (Yes. People can have different opinions and still consult with courtesy.)

6. Can people live far apart and still be unified?
   (Yes. Family and friends might live in different parts of the world.)

7. It is possible to be unified with people we don't even know?
   (Yes. Bahá'ís around the world are all working together for the same goals.)

8. No two people are exactly alike. Why do you think God made us all different?

The Power of Unity – Lesson #2

CRAFT ACTIVITIES

Craft activities are designed to reinforce material presented during the class sessions. For a weekend retreat, there may only be time for one or two crafts. For an ongoing class, you might choose a different craft each time. Another option is to prepare a separate table for each craft and have each child choose one to start. If their first choice is full, they can select another station. When they have completed a project and cleaned up their work area, they may assist others who need help, or move on to the next station. Remind children to label all projects with their names. Quiet music can be played in the background if desired.

(A) FLOWERS OF ONE GARDEN

(B) BRAIDED LANYARDS

(Can be used with lesson #1 on unity)

(C) LEAF LAMINATES

(D) DIVERSITY STREAMERS

The Power of Unity – Lesson #2

FLOWERS OF ONE GARDEN

> "The world of humanity is like a garden and the various races are the flowers..."
> ('Abdu'l-Bahá, Foundations of World Unity, p. 34)

Materials

- ☐ Scissors
- ☐ Glue sticks
- ☐ Old magazines with pictures of people
- ☐ Construction paper (¼ sheets and full sheets in different colors)
- ☐ White poster board (approx. 11 x 14 inches or 28 x 36 cm.)
  (Four can be cut from 22 x 28-inch standard poster board.)
- ☐ Circle patterns in different sizes
  (e.g., small plastic lids or ribbon spools to trace around)
- ☐ Sponge pieces cut into 1-inch squares, ¼-inch or 6 mm thick (optional)
- ☐ Pencils, colored markers and black permanent markers
- ☐ Yarn in different colors (optional)

Instructions

1. Search through magazines and tear out 5-6 pages with photos of people's faces.
   (Look for people of different colors.)

2. Using one of the circle patterns, trace a circle around each face.
   Then carefully cut out the circle.

3. Glue each face in the center of ¼ sheet of construction paper.
   Use a different color of paper for each face.

4. Draw flower petals around each face and cut out the flower.

5. Glue the flowers onto the poster board, or for a 3-D effect, first glue the
   flowers onto the sponge squares, so the photos stand out from the background.

6. Add your name, and decorate the page if desired:
   - Add a quote or heading.
   - Draw leaves and stems.
   - Glue a ring of yarn around each face circle.

The Power of Unity – Lesson #2

Samples of the "Flowers of One Garden" collage

The Power of Unity – Lesson #2

LANYARDS

> *"We must all strive with heart and soul until we have the reality of unity in our midst, and as we work, so will strength be given unto us."*
>
> ('Abdu'l-Bahá, Paris Talks, p. 54)

A lanyard is a concrete example of the strength that comes from unity.

Materials

- ☐ Lanyard (flat plastic lacing, also called craft lace, gimp or boondoggle)
- ☐ Scissors
- ☐ Ruler or tape measure
- ☐ Lanyard hooks, swivels or key rings
- ☐ Nails or pushpins (optional)
- ☐ Paper clips

Lanyard supplies can be found at craft stores or online, e.g., www.guildcraftinc.com > type "boondoggle" in the search box; or www.tandyleatherfactory.com > search for "craft lace."

Projects: Children can make a variety of lanyard projects including key chains, bike streamers, shoe bobs, bracelets, barrettes and zipper pulls. Different stitches can be used to make the project: square, circle, butterfly, triangle, spiral, braid, diamond, brick, twist, corkscrew, chainlink and more. Children should start with a basic box or square stitch.

Lanyard earrings

Online Instructions

- www.youtube.com > enter "boondoggle square stitch" in the search box
- www.boondoggleman.com > click on "square stitch"

The Boondoggle Man also describes more advanced stitches, and has photos of completed projects. Click on "Some Ideas."

Tips

1. For most beginning projects, you will need two strands of lanyard the same length.
2. Use 12 inches (30 cm) of lanyard for each inch (2.5 cm) of final project. For example, a 3-inch (7.5 cm) key chain would need two 3-foot (1 meter) strands of lanyard.
3. Measure carefully to avoid wasting material or running out in the middle of a project.
4. Warm the plastic lace in the sun to make it more flexible and easier to work with.
5. Loop both strands through a paper clip, key ring or lanyard hook before you begin.
6. Find the centers and make a starter stitch (see instructions online).
7. Hook the lanyard around a nail or pushpin to hold it while you work.
8. Pull stitches tight, with the same amount of tension for each stitch.
9. Don't pull too tight or the lanyard could break.
10. If you stop before your project is completed, attach a paper clip after the last stitch to keep the ends in place.
11. End the project with a finishing stitch.

The Power of Unity – Lesson #2

LEAF LAMINATES

"Ye are all the leaves of one tree."
(Tablets of Bahá'u'lláh, p. 27)

Materials for laminate

- ❏ Newspaper
- ❏ Wax paper sheets, pre-cut to fit frame (approx. 8½ x 10 inches or 22 x 28 cm)
- ❏ Fresh leaves (gathered by the children)
- ❏ Confetti, glitter, bits of colored paper (optional)
- ❏ Iron
- ❏ Scissors

Materials for frame

- ❏ Construction paper
- ❏ Ruler
- ❏ Pencil
- ❏ Craft knife or scissors
- ❏ Cutting board (optional)
- ❏ Clear tape
- ❏ Permanent marker
- ❏ Glue stick

Instructions

1. Spread two sheets of newspaper on table and place one sheet of wax paper on top.

2. Arrange the leaves and any glitter, confetti or other items on the wax paper.

> **Important:** Do not place leaves near edge. Leave a one-inch margin to obtain a good seal.

3. Place another sheet of wax paper on top of the leaves and cover this with two more sheets of newspaper.

4. Press the top of the newspaper with a warm iron (polyester setting) until the wax paper melts together. An iron that is too hot may damage the leaves and prevent the wax paper from sticking. Children should be carefully supervised for this step, or an adult should use the iron.

5. Remove the wax paper "sandwich" and trim any rough edges with a scissors. The sandwich should be just a little larger than the frame window.

For best results, select flat leaves with interesting edges and without bulky stems.

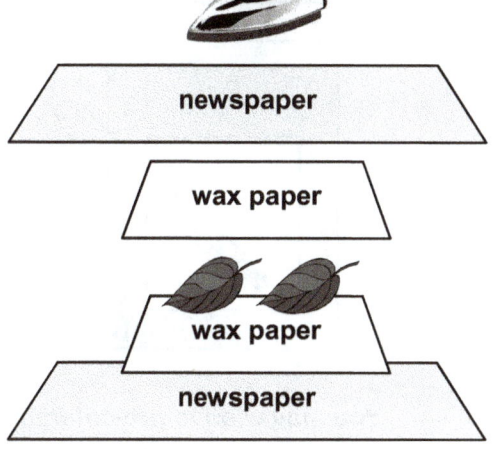

Making a Frame

1. Select two sheets of construction paper (any color), and stack them one on top of the other.

2. Using the ruler and pencil, draw lines about ¾-inch (2 cm) in from the bottom and side edges of the construction paper, and about 2½ inches (6 cm) from the top.

3. Place both sheets of paper on the cutting board, and using the craft knife, carefully cut out a rectangle along the lines just drawn. Cut through both sheets of paper at once. Be careful not to cut through to the edges. (Children will need careful supervision or assistance.)

> Note: A scissors can be used instead of the craft knife and cutting board. If using a scissors, start by poking a hole in the center of the paper, then cutting out to the lines.

4. Remove the inner rectangles, and tape the leaf sandwich inside the resulting window. Put tape on the side of the frame with the pencil lines. ⟶

5. Attach the back of the frame using the glue stick.

6. On the front side, use the marker to write a quote or heading. For a more finished look, neatly print the heading on a separate piece of paper and glue it onto the frame.

7. Display the finished project in a window and watch the light shine through.

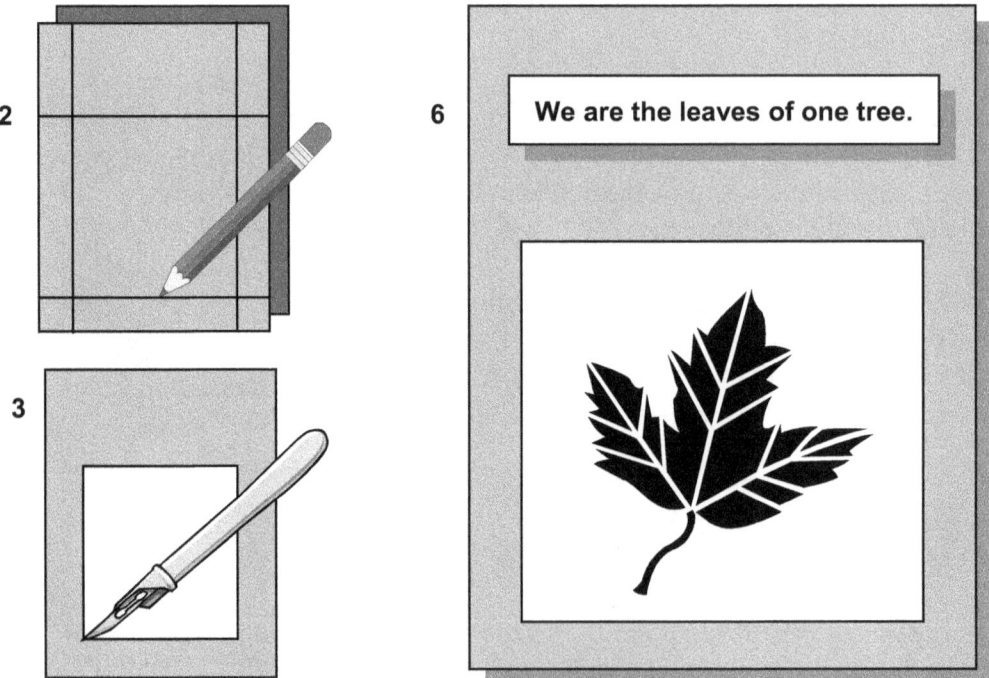

You may wish to pre-cut frames for younger children. A simple frame can also be made by gluing strips of construction paper along the edges of the wax paper.

The Power of Unity – Lesson #2

Sample "Leaf Laminate" with frame

Bahá'í Children's Classes and Retreats: Theme 5, p. 53

The Power of Unity – Lesson #2

DIVERSITY STREAMER

"You should strive to create a Bahá'í community which will offer to the entire world a vibrant model of unity in diversity."

(The Universal House of Justice, Ridván 153, 1996, to Bahá'ís of North America)

Materials

- ❏ Clean, empty tin can
- ❏ Awl (or hammer and large nail)
- ❏ Ribbon in different colors and widths
- ❏ Scissors
- ❏ Masking tape
- ❏ Duct tape
- ❏ Contact paper (solid color or wood-grain)
- ❏ Assortment of stickers
- ❏ Thin chain, thick yarn, or strand of plastic beads for hanging the can (approx. 1 yard or meter)
- ❏ Paper clip, pipe cleaner or small piece of wire for attaching chain

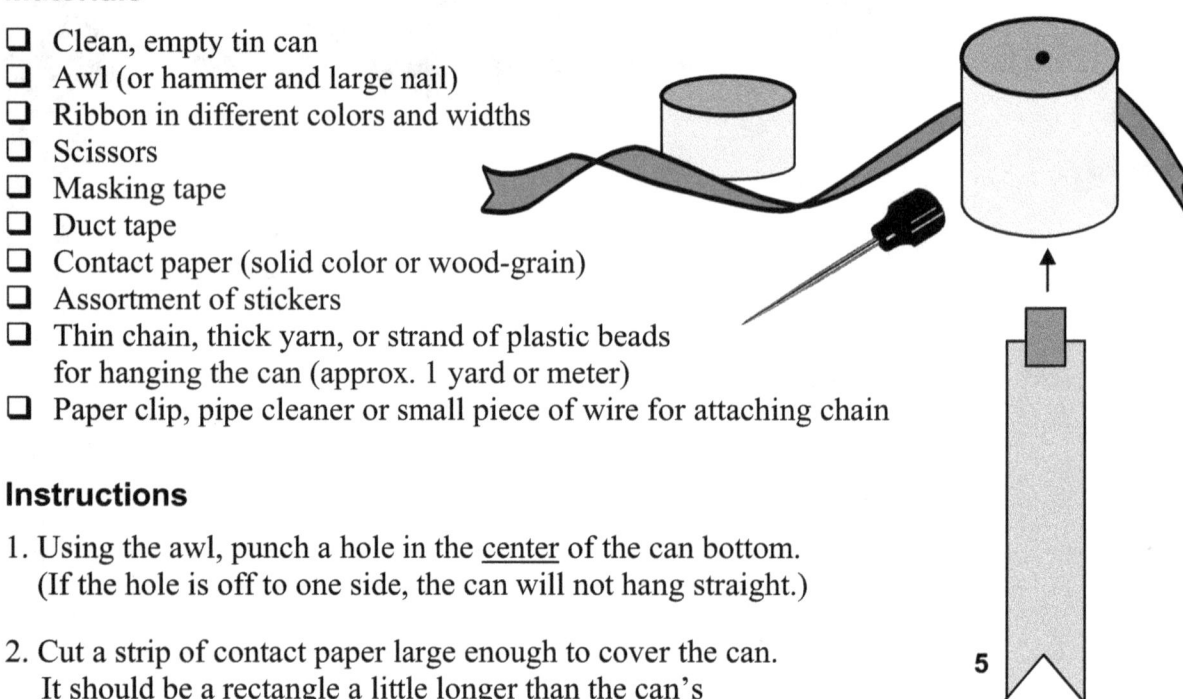

Instructions

1. Using the awl, punch a hole in the <u>center</u> of the can bottom. (If the hole is off to one side, the can will not hang straight.)

2. Cut a strip of contact paper large enough to cover the can. It should be a rectangle a little longer than the can's circumference, and a little taller than the can's height.

3. Carefully apply the contact paper to the outside of the can, slowly peeling off the backing and smoothing out bubbles as you go. Overlap edges around the side, and trim off excess paper at the top with a scissors.

4. Cut about 10 lengths of ribbon, each approx. 18 inches (46 cm.)

5. Trim one end of each ribbon into a "V" shape.

6. Using a small piece of masking tape, tape the straight edge of one ribbon to the inside of the can.

7. Continue adding ribbons all around the inside of the can. Ribbons should touch each other side-to-side with no gaps. When finished, reinforce with strips of duct tape.

8. Decorate the can with stickers if desired.

9. To hang, thread a length of yarn or chain up through the hole in the bottom of the can. Hold it in place with a knot, a paper clip, pipe cleaner, short piece of wire or tape.

Bahá'í Children's Classes and Retreats: Theme 5, p. 54

The Power of Unity – Lesson #2

Kierra with her diversity streamer

The Power of Unity – Lesson #2

MATERIALS NEEDED

- ❏ White board, easel, markers, eraser
- ❏ Folders with song sheets and page of quotations for each student **A**
- ❏ Packet of readings on "The Power of Unity" **A**
- ❏ "Unity in Diversity" handout (included with this lesson)
- ❏ Tree branch with leaves, a basket of fruit, and a vase with diverse flowers. (A picture will suffice if the real item is not available.)
- ❏ Felt lesson on "The Eye" (script and patterns included)
- ❏ Felt board (with a second easel for convenience if available)
- ❏ Cards or list of machines for activity #7
- ❏ A copy of "Unity in Diversity Discussion Questions" for each group facilitator
- ❏ Materials for craft activities (see separate lists), sample of each project, and page of instructions for the assistant at each station
- ❏ References for teachers (included at the end of this manual)

A. Included in the Handouts section of this teacher's guide.

LESSON #3

The Colors We Are

The Power of Unity – Lesson #3

The Colors We Are

Objectives: Students will be able to:
- Explain why we need skin and how we get our skin color.
- Recognize that our system of color-labeling people is not accurate.
- Choose a name for their own skin color.
- Recognize that we are each special in many different ways.

Before class, prepare all instructional materials on the list at the end of this lesson. Write the words "pigment" and "melanin" on the board. Set up craft area. Orient volunteers. Distribute folders and pencils to each student.

---

1. MEMORY QUOTES (5-10 min.)

Ask for a few volunteers to recite from memory the quotes learned during previous lessons:

- *"So powerful is the light of unity that it can illuminate the whole earth."* (Bahá'u'lláh)
- *"Regard ye not one another as strangers. Ye are the fruits of one tree, and the leaves of one branch."* ('Abdu'l-Bahá)

If there is time and interest, have students locate quote #14 on their quotations page: *"God does not look at colors; He looks at the hearts."* Write the quote on the board and follow the memorization process outlined in Lesson #1 (p. 27).

2. SKIN COLOR DEMO (10-15 min.)

Ask the class:

> This demonstration is based on a talk given many years ago by Hand of the Cause of God William Sears.

- How many human races are there? *(That's right, only one!)*
- Just because we're part of one human family, it doesn't mean we all have the same color hair, eyes or skin. Can you name some common skin colors? *(Accept all reasonable responses, including red and yellow which are discussed below.)*

   A. Have five volunteers line up in front of the room, each holding up a large close-up color photograph of a face (see list of materials at end of lesson).

   B. Give five sheets of colored construction paper to a sixth volunteer, and have her/him match one sheet to each face, according to the colors we commonly use for people (see chart below). The sixth volunteer should give the matching paper to the person holding the relevant photo. Have them hold it next to the face in the photograph so it can easily be compared to the actual skin color.

Bahá'í Children's Classes and Retreats: Theme 5, p. 58

The Power of Unity – Lesson #3

black	African
white	European
red	American Indian
yellow	Asian
brown	Hispanic/Latino

C. For each photograph, ask the children if the paper color truly matches the skin color. *(Guide them to recognize that American Indians are not really red; people of Asian descent are not really yellow; people of European descent are not really white, etc.)*

D. Then take the light brown ("tan") construction paper and hold it next to each face, one by one. Ask the class which is closer to the actual skin color: tan or the shade assigned by society? *(While some of us have very dark or very light skin, most people come in different shades of tan.)*

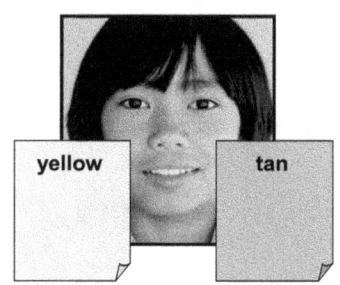
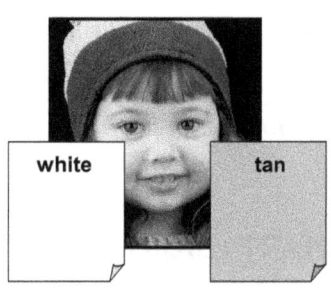

Tip: Use light brown for a better match.

E. Ask the children what we can learn from this demonstration.
(Our system of labeling people by color is not accurate!)

3. COLORS OF OUR WORLD (2 min.)

Explain to the class that today, we're going to find out what colors we really are!

- There are many types of pigments or colorings, that brighten our world.
- **Carotene** pigment makes carrots and pumpkins orange.
- **Chlorophyll** pigment makes leaves and grass green.
- **Hemoglobin** pigment makes our blood red.
- And **melanin** pigment makes our skin brown.
  All people have melanin in their skin.*
  Melanin protects us from the sun's harmful rays.

* Note to teacher: People with a rare form of albinism are unable to produce melanin.

While speaking, hold up a large color picture of each item. See examples below.

The Power of Unity – Lesson #3

4. HOW WE GET OUR SKIN COLOR (15-20 min.)

Using the book, *All the Colors We Are*, read the story while showing children the pictures. (See ordering information at the end of this lesson.)

As you read, have children suggest answers to the questions in the text:

- *What color is your skin?*
- *How do you think we get our own special color of skin?*
- *Do you think your ancestors came from a very warm, sunny place?*
- *Or did they come from a cooler place with less sunshine?*

Write their answers on the board. The words "pigment" and "melanin" should already be on the board so children can see how they are spelled.

After reading the story, ask the questions found at the end of this lesson for activity #4.

5. CLASS FEATURES CHART (20-30 min.)

Be sure group leaders are ready with their instructions and blank charts (found at the end of this lesson), paint samples, pencils and mirrors.

Hold up a "pigment poster" depicting various skin shades, and explain to the children that we are going to learn about our own special colors. Divide the class into small groups of four or five, and assign an assistant to each group. Groups can move to another room or outside if desired. Give them about 15 minutes to work. Then call them back together and post their charts on the wall. Share a few of the descriptions, then ask:

- What do we need skin for?
  (It keeps our bones and muscles in, keeps the germs out, protects us from the sun, allows us to give off heat by sweating, contains our sense of touch, pain, etc. And as one child explained it, "So we don't leak!")

- What does this activity tell us about the way we look?
  (We all have the same basic parts, with some variations.)

Note: If the teacher shows enthusiasm for this activity, the children will likely feel excited as well and will be eager to begin their investigations. If the teacher is uneasy or anxious, the children will receive a negative message about skin color, and may be more hesitant.

The Power of Unity – Lesson #3

6. HOORAY FOR SKIN (5-10 min.)

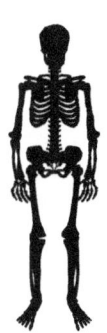

Read this poem aloud, while the children follow along. The handout is in the "Power of Unity" packet in their folders. A copy is also included with this lesson for convenience. Ask them what they think the poem means.

7. SONG: "Good Neighbors Come in All Colors" (5-10 min.)

Have students take out their song sheets and sing along. Ask the music coordinator for assistance if needed.

8. PERSONAL POSTER (45-60 min.)

This project (see instructions at end of lesson) is designed to reinforce material presented during class and to encourage children to celebrate their own diversity. Show them a sample poster beforehand, and display their work when they have finished. If there is time and interest, the children can share *"What my picture means to me,"* and *"What I learned about my classmates"* – either in small groups or as a whole class.

*After the children clean up their work area,
dismiss them for outdoor activities.*

* * * * *

The Power of Unity – Lesson #3

Questions for activity #4

How We Get Our Skin Color

1. Can skin change its color? *(Yes, in the sun it can get darker, turn pink or red, or burn.)*

2. Long ago, when groups of people lived in the same part of the world for thousands of years, what happened to their skin in places like Nigeria, West Africa, which is close to the Equator and receives a lot of direct sun? *(Their skin gradually became darker.)*

3. Why? *(To protect people by blocking the sun's rays.)*

4. What happened to peoples' skin in places like Sweden, where the sun is much less intense? *(It gradually got lighter to let in more of the sun's rays.)*

Using a flashlight to represent the sun, shine it on the globe to show that the light is more direct, and thus more intense, near the equator, and less intense near the poles.

5. Where do you think the ancestors of these people may have lived? And these people? *(Show photos of people whose ancestors came from very warm and very cold climates.)*

6. What happens if we get too much sun? *(Sunburn, heatstroke, skin cancer.)*

7. Too little sun? *(Our body won't produce enough vitamin D, so we can't absorb calcium, leading to rickets* and weak bones.)*

8. In order to be healthy, humans need just the right amount of sun. God designed the pigment in our skin to adapt to the sun's rays. In the past, because people had different skin colors, scientists thought we were separate races. But Bahá'u'lláh has told us that we are all members of one human race. And scientists have finally proven that today!

> * <u>Teacher's Note</u>: Rickets is a severe and prolonged vitamin D deficiency that leads to softening and weakening of the bones in children. Vitamin D helps the body absorb calcium which children need to build strong bones. Rickets can also be caused by lack of exposure to sunlight, which stimulates the body to make vitamin D. Signs and symptoms of rickets include bowed legs, leg fractures and impaired growth. (www.mayoclinic.com)

The Power of Unity – Lesson #3

Instructions for activity #5

Class Features Activity

Materials needed: Mirrors, paint samples, class features chart, pencils

> ***Instructions for group leaders:*** *Gather your small group and find a quiet place to work. Your job is to encourage all the children to participate. Do not allow them to laugh at or tease each other. You will have about 15 minutes to work.*

1. Ask children to study the paint samples and to choose the one that most closely matches their own skin color. Practice saying the colors out loud.

   (Children can decide to use the labels on the paint samples as their skin color names, or they can choose other names. This activity focuses on the beauty of skin color. It helps the children to realize that they each have their own special color, and it empowers them to decide how they wish to be called. As the group leader, you should participate too.)

2. Work with students to fill in the features chart (see sample below).

Name	Eye color	Skin color	Hair length, color, texture
Maria	brown	gingersnap	long, reddish, straight
Marcus	black	caramel	short, black, curly
Lua	blue	peach	medium, blonde, wavy

Hair can be straight, wavy, curly, twisty, frizzy, with springy coils, loose curls, and more...

3. After completing the chart, ask the children: "What do we need skin for?"

4. Return to the classroom with your group and post your chart on the wall.

The Power of Unity – Lesson #3

For activity #5

Class Features Chart

Name	Eye color	Skin color	Hair length, color, texture

The Power of Unity – Lesson #3

HOORAY FOR SKIN
by Susan Engle

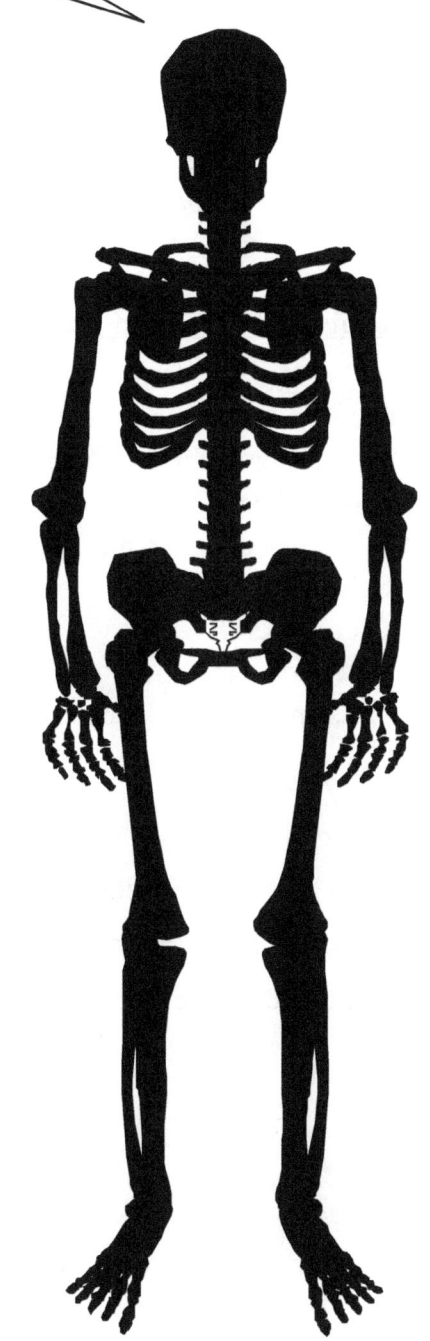

Rejoice and celebrate the skin
That keeps the veins and muscles in,
That keeps the cold and germies out.
That is what skin is all about.

Suppose, when God created skin,
He turned the skinside outside-in.
So when you talk to Mrs. Jones,
Your eyes meet over fat and bones,
And tissues, blue and white and red,
That stretch from toe to hand to head.
It makes me glad to have a skin
To keep the outside boneside-in.

Now there are folks who would be mad
If our insides were all they had
To tell all kinds of folks apart.
Maybe they'd learn to read the heart
Instead of judging from a hue
If one man's false and one man's true.

Let's all join hands and feast our eyes
On skins of every shape and size,
Of every tone of gold or white,
Of luscious black, of dark or light,
Of every shade that folks come in.
Rejoice and celebrate the skin.

© 1986, Susan Engle. Used with permission.

The Power of Unity – Lesson #3

Personal Poster
A Celebration of Our Diversity

> "If you meet those of a different race and colour from yourself...think of them as different coloured roses growing in the beautiful garden of humanity, and rejoice to be among them."
>
> ('Abdu'l-Bahá, Paris Talks, p. 53)

Have children finish the writing and tracing activities before you set out the paint at each table. When done, they should clean up the workspace and hang up their posters for display. They will have about 45 minutes to work.

Materials for Writing and Tracing

- ❏ "I Am Special" form
- ❏ Lined paper (trimmed to same size as form)
- ❏ Marker for printing first name
- ❏ Pens and pencils
- ❏ Cardstock or watercolor paper
- ❏ Scissors
- ❏ Glue sticks
- ❏ File folders in various colors (these can be turned inside out to hide brand names), or use poster board (approx.12 x 17 inches or 30 x 44 cm.)

Instructions for Writing and Tracing

1. Fill in the "I Am Special" form or write your own text on lined paper.

2. Trace your hand and wrist on the cardstock, then carefully cut out the drawing.

3. Glue the text page onto one side of the folder.

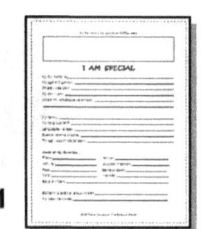

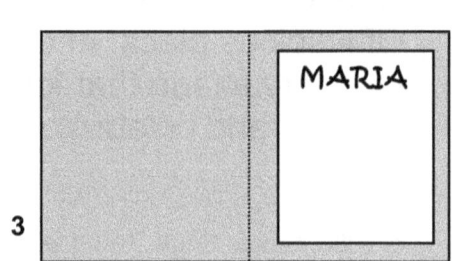

Bahá'í Children's Classes and Retreats: Theme 5, p. 66

The Power of Unity – Lesson #3

# Painting the Hand
for Your Personal Poster

Materials for Painting

- ❑ Newspaper or tarp to protect table
- ❑ Extra sheet of paper to place under each painting
- ❑ Hand cutouts from tracing activity (above)
- ❑ Tempera or acrylic craft paints, preferably in squeeze bottles (black, white, red, yellow, blue)
- ❑ Sturdy paper plates for mixing colors
- ❑ Paint brushes
- ❑ Water cups for rinsing brushes
- ❑ Paper towels for clean up
- ❑ Tacks or clothesline to hang pictures for display

Tip: Have the children experiment, but don't do it for them. Provide guidance by letting them start with one color, then ask:
Do you think it needs more blue or red?
Do you need to add a lighter or darker color to match your skin?

Instructions for Painting

1. Set paints out in center of table, and give each child a mixing plate, brush and water cup.

2. Put small dabs of various colors on each child's plate, and assist them to mix the colors until they find one that closely matches their skin.

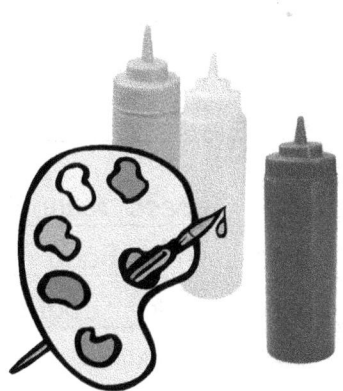

Tip: red + yellow + blue = brown.

3. The matching color should be used to paint their hand cutout.

4. When dry, glue the cutout onto the folder and hang in the craft display area.

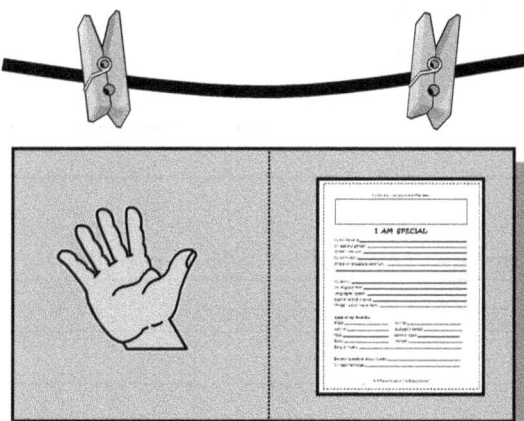

If the children wish, as a group project, they can paint additional hands and arrange these around a quotation on a large poster board.

Bahá'í Children's Classes and Retreats: Theme 5, p. 67

The Power of Unity – Lesson #3

Sample form for Personal Poster – activity #8

Print first name in box using large CAPITAL letters

I AM SPECIAL

My full name is: Maria Elena Garcia

My age and gender: 9 years old, female

Where I was born: Yakima, Washington

My skin color: Ancient gold

Where my ancestors were from: Bolivia – Sweden – France – USA

My family: Teresa, Manuel, Juan, Lily, Lilita, me (Maria Elena)

My religious faith: Bahá'í

Languages I speak: English and Spanish

Special talents or skills: Music (flute)

Things I would like to learn: French and guitar

Some of my favorites…

Place: Chuck-E-Cheese   Animal: Romeo & Juliet (my parakeets)

Activity: soccer   Subject in school: recess

Food: ice cream   Game or sport: soccer

Color: red   Holiday: Christmas

Song or music: rock music

Something special about myself: I can curl my tongue

My best memories: When I visited my cousins in California

Bahá'í Children's Classes and Retreats: Theme 5, p. 68

The Power of Unity – Lesson #3

Print first name in box using large CAPITAL letters

I AM SPECIAL

My full name is: _____

My age and gender: _____

Where I was born: _____

My skin color: _____

Where my ancestors were from:_____
_____

My family: _____

My religious faith: _____

Languages I speak: _____

Special talents or skills: _____

Things I would like to learn: _____

Some of my favorites…

Place: _____ Animal:_____

Activity: _____ Subject in school:_____

Food:_____ Game or sport:_____

Color:_____ Holiday:_____

Song or music:_____

Something special about myself:_____

My best memories: _____

BCR Theme 5 – Lesson #3 – Personal Poster

Make one copy of this page for each student, and trim on dotted lines.

The Power of Unity – Lesson #3

MATERIALS NEEDED

> Note to Teachers: At first glance, the long list of instructional materials below might seem overwhelming. However most of these items are included with the lesson or are readily available for download from the UnityWorks website. For the remaining items, once obtained, they can be re-used for many years.
>
> The wide variety of materials also makes the lessons more memorable and enjoyable for the children, increases understanding and retention of the concepts, and allows for diverse learning styles.

- ❑ White board, easel, markers, eraser and pencils
- ❑ Folders with song sheets and page of quotations for each student
- ❑ Packet of readings on "The Power of Unity"[A]
- ❑ Dictionary, globe, and large world map if available

- ❑ **Skin Color Demo:** Materials for activity #2
    - Five sheets of construction paper (black, white, red, yellow, light brown)
    - Five large close-up color photos of diverse people to symbolically match the construction paper colors above (i.e., African, European, Native American, Asian, Hispanic/Latino)[B]

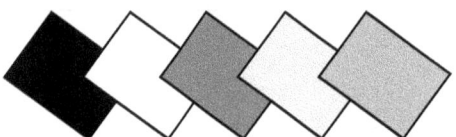

- ❑ **Colors of Our World:** Four large color pictures for activity #3 [C]
    - Bright orange pumpkin
    - Dark green leaf
    - Red heart
    - Photo or collage of faces of diverse people

- ❑ **How We Get Our Skin Color:** Materials for activity #4
    - The book, *All the Colors We Are.*[D]
    - Page of questions (included here)
    - Bright flashlight and globe
    - Photos of people whose ancestors came from very warm climates and very cold climates (a few of each)[B]

Bahá'í Children's Classes and Retreats: Theme 5, p. 70

The Power of Unity – Lesson #3

- ❑ **Class Features Chart:** Materials for activity #5
  - Instruction page and blank features chart for each group leader (included)
  - Flesh-tone paint chip samples (one set per group)^E
  - Small hand mirrors (one for every 2-3 students)
  - Tape or tacks for posting class features charts on the wall
  - Pigment Poster^F

  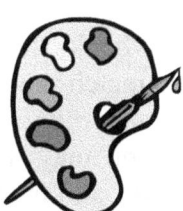

  For photographs of different hair types:
  - www.curls.biz/curly-hair-type-guide.html

  For a discussion of the term "nappy hair"
  - www.nappyhairaffair.com
  - www.adversity.net/special/nappy_hair.htm
  - www.carolivia.org/nappyhair

- ❑ *Hooray for Skin* poem (included)

- ❑ **Personal Poster:** Materials for activity #8
  - Page of instructions for each assistant (included)
  - Craft supplies for making posters (see separate list)
  - Blank "I Am Special" forms (one for each student)
  - Skin color reference charts (optional) ^G
  - Sample Personal Poster

- ❑ References for teachers (included at the end of this manual)

A. Included in the Handouts section of this teacher's guide

B. Some of these photographs may already be posted around the room from a previous class. They are also available as part of the download packet for this teacher's guide at: **www.UnityWorksStore.com.** Click on Children's Classes > Power of Unity > student handouts.

Additional images of people can be found in Bahá'í booklets on race unity, at teacher supply stores in the social studies section, from educational textbook publishers under classroom posters, in multicultural calendars, clip art, and National Geographic Magazine: www.nationalgeographic.com.

The Power of Unity – Lesson #3

C. These pictures are available as part of the download packet for this teacher's guide. Similar images can be found in most clip art programs or on the Internet, but may be subject to copyright.

One excellent source of online images is **www.google.com.** For example, click on "Images" and type "pumpkin" in the search box. A variety of pumpkins will appear. Double-click on the image you wish to use. Next, click on "See full size image," right-click on the image, then "Save Picture As." Give the file a name and save it to your desktop or other location. It will then be available for editing and printing. Images can be enlarged, mounted, laminated or displayed in a plastic page protector.

D. *All The Colors We Are / Todos los Colores de Nuestra Piel: The Story of How We Get Our Skin Color,* by Katie Kissinger with photographs by Wernher Krutein, is published by Redleaf Press, MN (www.redleaf press.org), ISBN: 0-934140-80-4. It is also distributed by www.amazon.com and may be available from your local library or bookstore.

E. Bring the above book, *All the Colors We Are,* to the paint store and ask for free paint chip samples to match the various skin tones. Choose paint samples with inviting names, e.g., *peachy cream, cinnamon swirl* and *sunny gold*, rather than *Tagsdale Linen* or *Rio Grande Mud*. You may need to select samples from different brands. Choose 15-20 colors for each set, and make a separate set for each group of students.

F. A sample *Pigment Poster* can be found in the download packet for this teacher's guide. If preferred, you can make your own poster by cutting up extra paint samples and arranging the pieces in a design to illustrate the beauty of our diverse skin tones. Glue your design onto tag board or laminate for durability. Students can also make their own posters (see page 103 for instructions).

G. Skin color reference charts from the book, *How to Paint Skin Tones,* are available online at: <http://slappingpaint.net/JN_creatingfleshtones.htm>. The charts show how to blend different paint colors to create specific skin tones.

* * * * *

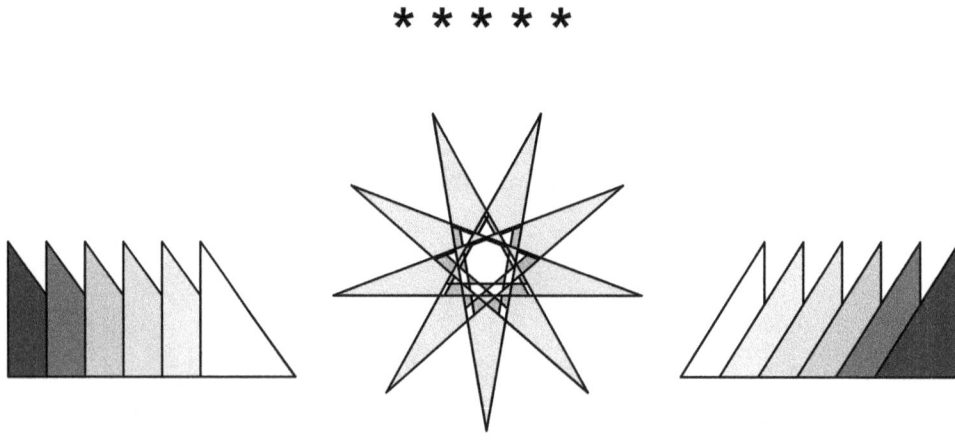

LESSON #4

Overcoming Prejudice

The Power of Unity – Lesson #4

Overcoming Prejudice

Objectives: Students will be able to:
- Name some of the barriers to unity, including prejudice.
- Define prejudice and describe some of its effects.
- Demonstrate positive responses to putdowns and biased remarks.
- Develop and role play various approaches to creating unity in their own families, schools and communities.

Before class, prepare all instructional materials on the list at the end of this lesson. Write the questions for activity #6 on a separate board or poster for ready reference. Set up felt board. Orient assistants. Distribute folders, markers and pens.

1. MEMORY QUOTES (5-10 min.)

Ask the class:

- What is one of the most important teachings of Bahá'u'lláh? *(Unity)*

Then ask for a few volunteers to recite the quotes learned during previous lessons:

- *"So powerful is the light of unity that it can illuminate the whole earth." (Bahá'u'lláh)*
- *"Regard ye not one another as strangers. Ye are the fruits of one tree, and the leaves of one branch." ('Abdu'l-Bahá)*
- *"God does not look at colors; He looks at the hearts." ('Abdu'l-Bahá)*

2. BRIDGES AND BARRIERS (5-10 min.)

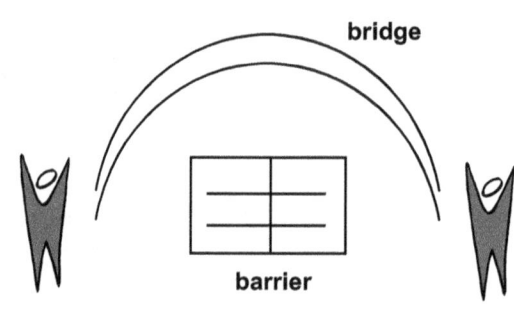

Illustrate on the board as you explain:

Sometimes our words and actions can be **barriers** to unity—like walls keeping people apart. And sometimes our words and actions can be like **bridges** of understanding—bonds connecting people's hearts.

A. Distribute one red card and one green card* to each child. Explain that red means *stop* and represents a brick in the wall. Green means *go* and represents a piece of the bridge.

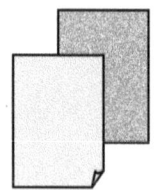

> * Note: Use 3x5 index cards or other sturdy paper.
> If red and green are not available, use two other colors.

Bahá'í Children's Classes and Retreats: Theme 5, p. 74

The Power of Unity – Lesson #4

B. On the red cards, ask students to write one thing that is a barrier to unity (e.g., backbiting, prejudice, name calling, disrespect, lies). They should print legibly and large, and check with their neighbors to insure that most cards have different items. Offer to assist with spelling as necessary.

C. On the green cards, have students write one thing that builds bridges between people (e.g., honesty, kindness, cooperation, sharing, helpfulness, fairness, service, love).

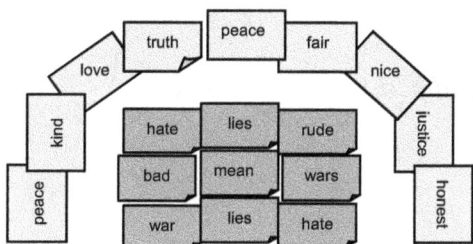

D. With the help of an assistant, have students tape their barrier words onto the classroom wall in the shape of a brick wall. Next, have them tape their bridge words in the shape of a bridge crossing over the wall (see illustration at left). Then read all the cards out loud.

Tip: Use a large bulletin board with tacks or pushpins if wall space is not available.

3. **PREJUDICE** (5-10 min.)

Write the word "prejudice" on the board and ask the following questions:

- One of the biggest barriers to unity is **prejudice**. Does anyone know what prejudice is? *(Not liking people before you get to know them; pre-judging people in a bad way.)* It's easy to remember if you separate the word into two parts: **pre – judice** (pre-judge).

- Some people think that their skin color or race is the best, and they don't like people of a different race or color. That's called racial prejudice. They don't understand that God made us with different skin colors to protect us from the sun, or that there is really only one human race. Prejudice isn't very logical, is it!

  In addition to racial prejudice, what other types of prejudice can you think of?

Write their answers on the board. (Sex, age, religion, language, accent, country, how much money someone has, how much education, type of job, clothing, height, weight, etc.)

- How do you think people feel when others are prejudiced <u>against</u> them?
  (Sad, hurt, left out, angry, frustrated, etc.)

- How do you think people feel who <u>are</u> prejudiced? *(Superior, better than others.)*

- How do they act toward people they don't like? *(Unkind, rude, unfair, etc.)*

- How does prejudice stop people from reaching unity? *(It keeps people apart.)*

The Power of Unity – Lesson #4

4. THE SNEETCHES (15-20 min.)

This classic Dr. Seuss poem is about prejudice. An excerpt from the poem is included in the *Power of Unity* packet in the children's folders. Have children locate the handout. (A copy is included at the end of this lesson for convenience.) Show them a picture* of the Sneetches, and read the excerpt out loud with feeling while the children follow along.

Then ask the class:

- How were the Star-Belly Sneetches acting?
  (Better than everyone else, rude, mean, prejudiced.)

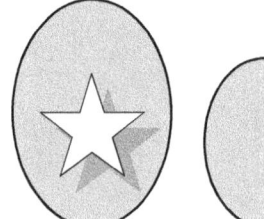

- Why? *(They had stars on their bellies, and thought this made them superior.)*

- Were they showing unity? *(No. Bahá'u'lláh said that prejudice is wrong. It is a barrier to unity, and we should get rid of it.)*

Have the children raise their hands to answer.

> Note to teachers: Sneetches are yellow bird-like cartoon creatures. Some of them have green stars on their bellies, while others do not. The stars become a symbol of privilege and discrimination.
>
> As a follow-up activity, you may wish to conduct the simulation exercise found on the Teaching Tolerance website: <www.tolerance.org/activity/anti-racism-activity-sneetches>.
>
> The purpose of the simulation is to help children understand the emotional impact of unfair practices. The activity will also help students understand that the goal is to change discriminatory attitudes and practices, and not the characteristics that make us different from one another.

*Pictures can be found online at: www.Google.com/images.
Type "sneetches" in the search box.*

5. PUTDOWNS (5-10 min.)

Distribute scratch paper to the class, and ask:

- Putdowns are another barrier to unity. Do you know what a putdown is?
  (A mean comment meant to hurt someone. Even if other people laugh and think it's funny, the person who is targeted still feels bad.)

- We're going to write down some common putdowns, not the worst ones you hear (we all know what they are), but some of the milder ones, e.g., stupid, ugly, weirdo, nerd. Write the words legibly on your scrap paper, and don't include your name.

This is a serious topic, and the teacher's attitude will influence how the children respond. Collect the papers, shuffle them, and read a few out loud.

Bahá'í Children's Classes and Retreats: Theme 5, p. 76

- Why do people use these putdowns?
  (To feel important, to gain control, to blame others, to fit in with the crowd...)

- What is it called when you use a putdown against someone who isn't there?
  (Backbiting)

- Do you think putdowns are okay?
  (No? I agree, so let's get rid of them!)

In front of the children, dramatically tear up all the papers and throw them away, to symbolically show that we don't want to use putdowns any more.

6. PERSONAL STORIES (20-30 min.)

Explain that we are going to share some personal stories about what it feels like when someone is prejudiced against you or isn't treating you nicely. Later we'll practice how to respond.

Divide the class into groups of three to discuss the questions below. The questions should already be listed on a separate board or poster. They are also included at the end of this lesson, so they can easily be copied if volunteers will be working with each group. Children might relate better to youth volunteers rather than adults for this activity.

A. How does it feel when someone is prejudiced against you or isn't treating you nicely?

B. Tell about a time when you were teased, put down, treated unfairly or left out. (2-3 min. each)
  - What happened?
  - How did you feel?
  - What would have helped?

C. Do you know of anyone in your life right now who might feel put down or left out?

D. What can you do to make that person feel included?

Tell the children not to share anything that should remain private.

Walk around the room to observe the group discussions, making sure everyone has a chance to participate. Be prepared in case there are a few tears.

If there is time to report back, have each group share a summary of their thoughts.

The Power of Unity – Lesson #4

7. PUT-UPS (5 min.)

Ask the class:

- If someone calls you a name, what do you think might happen if you call them a name too?

- How can you respond without putting them down?

- Let's also brainstorm some *"put-ups"*—nice things to say to help build people up, rather than putting them down.

Call on different students and write their suggestions on the board.

8. READING: "Dealing with Putdowns and Prejudice" (5-10 min.)

After brainstorming, have students read "Dealing with Putdowns and Prejudice," from the handout packet in their folders. A copy is also included with this lesson. Call on volunteers to read each section aloud, and encourage children to add their own ideas as well.

9. WORKSHEET AND SKITS: "Name It, Claim It" (15-20 min.)

"Name It, Claim It, Stop It" is another strategy for dealing with putdowns and prejudice. Have students locate the handout (in their *Power of Unity* packet) and choose a partner. They should read through the worksheet together and complete the exercises. Allow them about ten minutes to work. Then ask for a few **volunteers** to act out the example they have created.

As an additional activity, ask two students to perform the middle skit on their handout (below).

> **Person A:** "I don't like purple people. They're all stupid!"
>
> **Person B:**
> 1. "What you just said about purple people— that's prejudice."
> 2. "It makes me sad to hear you say things like that."
> 3. "Please don't talk that way around me."

Have them act it out a second time, but instead of one person standing up, ask two people to stand up and say "Stop!" Repeat with five people arising; then again with the entire class.

After the demonstration, ask Person A and Person B how they each felt when only one person stood up, and how they felt when everyone did. The more people who stand up for justice, the more power they will have. There is strength in unity.

The Power of Unity – Lesson #4

10. STORY: "The Black Rose" (30 min.)

If time allows, read and discuss the story of "The Black Rose" found at the end of this lesson. The story is an elegant example of how 'Abdu'l-Bahá responded to prejudice and showed unconditional love for all. Read the story as a whole class or appoint volunteers to work with the children in small groups. Have some chocolate candy ready after the story.

When sharing the story, explain that before Bahá'u'lláh passed away, He appointed His oldest son, 'Abdu'l-Bahá, as head of the Bahá'í Faith. Although not a Manifestation of God, 'Abdu'l-Bahá was a perfect example of His Father's teachings. 'Abdu'l-Bahá's entire life was a model of generosity, kindness, humility, love, and service to all. We can all look to His example of how a true believer should be.

11. CRAFT: Chocolate Roses (30-40 min.)

Craft activities are designed to reinforce material presented during the class. See instructions at the end of this lesson.

12. ROLE PLAYS: "Creating Unity" (40-60 min.)

Have students turn to the "Creating Unity" handout in their packets.

A. Explain that Bahá'u'lláh wants us to be unifiers, to build bridges and break down walls between people. In order to be successful, we can't just <u>believe</u> in unity. We have to <u>act</u> on our beliefs. These role plays will give us an opportunity to practice.

You can also develop your own role plays as appropriate for your students.

B. Divide the class into groups of 3-4, and put a volunteer in charge of each group.

C. Assign one or more role plays to each group. They will be performing these for the class. Give the groups about 15 minutes to prepare.

D. They should act out each role play twice: first in a negative way, and a second time, in a way that creates unity. After each group's performance, the children may wish to discuss alternative solutions to the one presented. Don't forget to applaud!

E. After all of the performances, ask the class to discuss what they have learned.

13. FELT LESSON: "Barriers into Bonds" (10-15 min.)

Present the felt lesson on "Barriers into Bonds" (see instructions at the end of this lesson). If there is time, ask several children if they would like to try it in front of the class without your help. They may also wish to volunteer for the children's performance.

14. MEMORY QUOTE: "In the sight of God..." (5-10 min.)

If there is time and interest, have students locate quote #17 on their quotations page.

Write these words on the board and follow the memorization process outlined in Lesson #1 (p. 27).

For a weekend retreat, you might have children only memorize one quote ("So powerful..." from lesson #1). For an ongoing class, they could memorize a different quote as part of each lesson.

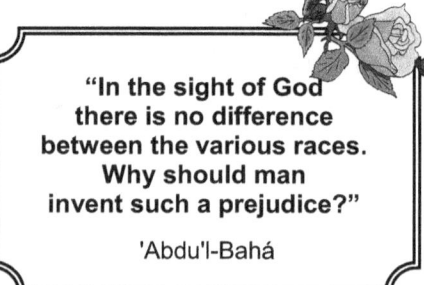

"In the sight of God there is no difference between the various races. Why should man invent such a prejudice?"

'Abdu'l-Bahá

15. SONG: "What Mankind Has to Learn" (10 min.)

Have students take out their song sheets and sing along. Ask the music coordinator for assistance if needed.

16. VISUALIZATION: "The Circle of Unity" (15 min.)

Take the children outside or into a large room and have them form a big circle. Enlist the help of several volunteers, and space them around the circle next to children who might need extra assistance.

Tell the class you are going to imagine together how it might feel if the world were truly unified. When the children are quiet, give each one a short length of red yarn and read the "The Circle of Unity" included at the end of this lesson. Modify the reading to fit the culture and life circumstances of your students.

"Bahá'u'lláh has drawn the circle of unity. He has made a design for the uniting of all the peoples, and for the gathering of them all under the shelter of the tent of universal unity."

'Abdu'l-Bahá, *Paris Talks*, p. 54

After the visualization, dismiss the children for outdoor activities.

* * * * *

Poem excerpt for activity #4

The Sneetches

From *The Sneetches and Other Stories* by Dr. Seuss.
TM & copyright © by Dr. Seuss Enterprises, L.P, 1953, 1954, 1961, renewed 1989.
Used by permission of Random House Children's Books, a division of Random House, Inc.

Now the Star-Belly Sneetches
Had bellies with stars.
The Plain-Belly Sneetches
Had none upon thars.

Those stars weren't so big
They were really so small.
You might think such a thing
Wouldn't matter at all.

But because they had stars
All the Star-Belly Sneetches
Would brag, "We're the best kind
Of Sneetches on beaches."

With their snoots in the air,
They would sniff and they'd snort
"We'll have nothing to do with
The Plain-Belly sort!"

And whenever they met some
When they were out walking,
They'd hike right on past them
Without even talking….

When the Star-Belly Sneetches
Had frankfurter roasts
Or picnics or parties
Or marshmallow toasts,

They never invited
The Plain-Belly Sneetches.
They left them out cold
In the dark on the beaches.

They kept them away.
Never let them come near.
And that's how they treated them
Year after year…

The Power of Unity – Lesson #4

Personal Stories

Instructions for group leaders for activity #6

> Gather your small group and find a quiet place. You will have about 15 minutes to work. Your job is to ask the questions below and encourage the children to share their thoughts and experiences. Do not require them to speak, but make sure everyone who wants to, has an opportunity. Be prepared in case there are a few tears.
>
> Do not allow the children to laugh at or tease each other. Take notes below. If there is time to report back, prepare the group to share a brief summary of their thoughts.

Explain that we are going to share some personal stories about what it **feels** like when someone is prejudiced against you or isn't treating you nicely. When someone else in our group is speaking, we should listen respectfully and try to understand what happened, even if we don't agree with it. Later we'll practice different ways to respond.

1. How does it feel when someone is prejudiced against you or isn't treating you nicely?

2. Tell about a time when you were teased, put down, treated unfairly or left out. (2-3 min. each)

   A. What happened?

   B. How did you feel?

   C. What would have helped?

3. Do you know of anyone in your life right now who might feel put down or left out?

4. What can you do to make that person feel included?

The Power of Unity – Lesson #4

Reading for activity #8

Dealing With
PUTDOWNS AND PREJUDICE

If someone calls you a name:
- Stay calm.
- Say, "I don't like it when you say that."
- Say, "That's mean. Please don't do it again!"
- Walk away.
- Tell some friends.
- Tell an adult.

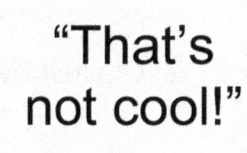
"That's not cool!"

Things to say to someone else who is called a name:
- It was wrong of her to say that about you. Are you okay?
- Can I help you report it to the teacher?
- Would you like to eat lunch with us from now on?

Ways to respond to prejudiced remarks:
- In our house, those words are not allowed.
- You're too nice a person to hurt someone like that.
- That's not okay. It's disrespectful to Native Americans.
- I don't like it when you say that. It's mean to girls.
- What makes you believe that about Arabs?
- Do you really mean what you said? Here's what I understood…
- I don't like that kind of joke. It puts down my family—the human family.

Try some *put-ups*:
- Nice to see you!
- Come and join us.
- You can do it.
- Good job!
- You look nice today.
- I like the way you shared your game.
- You were very helpful just now.
- Would you like to be friends?

The Power of Unity – Lesson #4

Worksheet for activity #9

NAME IT, CLAIM IT, STOP IT

Adapted from a workshop given by Peggy Federici, Camp Peace, Idaho

"Name It, Claim It, Stop It" is another strategy for dealing with putdowns and prejudice. When you hear a biased remark, you can respond with three simple statements:

1. Name the biased behavior.
2. Claim it by stating how it makes you feel.
3. Tell the person to stop.

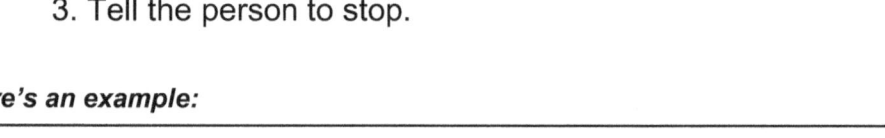

Here's an example:

Biased remark: "How many green people does it take to change a light bulb?"
Name It: "That's a racist joke."
Claim It: "I don't like it when you put down green people like that."
Stop It: "Please don't tell those jokes at our school."

See if you can label all three parts in the example below:

Biased remark: "I don't like purple people. They're all stupid!"

1. "What you just said about purple people— that's prejudice." _____
2. "It makes me sad to hear you say things like that." _____
3. "Please don't talk that way around me." _____

Now try your own example:

Biased remark: "_____"

Name It: _____
Claim It: _____
Stop It: _____

Practice with your partner and be ready to act out your example for the class.

The Power of Unity – Lesson #4

The Black Rose

Instructions for group leaders for activity #10

> Gather your small group and find a quiet place. You will have about 20 minutes to work. Your job is to read the story out loud, then ask the questions below. Encourage the children to share their thoughts. Do not allow them to laugh at or tease each other. Take notes, and if there is time to report back, prepare the group to share any insights or highlights from the story.

One day, when 'Abdu'l-Bahá was visiting a very poor section of New York, a large group of boys gathered around Him. Some threw sticks and called Him names. Mrs. Kinney, one of the local Bahá'ís who was with 'Abdu'l-Bahá, dropped behind to speak with the boys. She explained that He was a very Holy Man who had spent many years in prison because of His love for truth and for all people. She invited the boys to her house to personally meet 'Abdu'l-Bahá.

When they arrived, 'Abdu'l-Bahá was standing at the door. He welcomed each one, sometimes with a handshake, sometimes with an arm around a shoulder, but always with such smiles and laughter that it almost seemed He was a boy with them. The young visitors felt right at home.

One of the last to enter the room was a boy of African descent, about 13 years old. Because he was the only one in the group with very dark skin, he thought he might not be welcome. But when 'Abdu'l-Bahá saw the boy, His face lit up with a heavenly smile. He raised His hand in greeting and exclaimed in a loud voice so everyone could hear, that here was a black rose.

Suddenly, everyone was silent. The black child's face was shining with happiness and love. He had probably been called many things in his short life, but never a black rose. The other boys looked at him with new eyes.

'Abdu'l-Bahá had a large box of expensive chocolates brought in for the boys. He carried it around the room Himself, giving each boy a large handful of candy, with a word and a smile for everyone. Then He set the box down and picked out a very dark piece of chocolate.

He looked at it for a moment and then at the boys who were watching Him intently. Without a word 'Abdu'l-Bahá walked across the room to where the black boy was sitting, and with a piercing glance that swept the group, laid the dark chocolate against the black cheek.

The Power of Unity – Lesson #4

'Abdu'l-Bahá's face was radiant as He laid His arm around the shoulder of the boy. That radiance seemed to fill the room. No words were necessary to convey His meaning, and there was no doubt that all of the boys understood.

Not only was the boy a black flower, but also a black sweet. You eat chocolates and find them good: perhaps you would also find this black brother of yours good – once you taste his sweetness.

Again the room fell silent, and the boy himself gazed at 'Abdu'l-Bahá with such love in his eyes that he seemed transformed. The reality of his being had been brought to the surface and the angel he really was, revealed.

To the few Bahá'ís in the room, the scene brought visions of a new world in which every soul would be treated as a child of God.

(Adapted from Howard Colby Ives, *Portals to Freedom*, p. 65-67)

Study Questions

1. What was 'Abdu'l-Bahá doing when he met the group of boys?

2. Why do you think the boys threw sticks and called 'Abdu'l-Bahá names?

3. Who was Mrs. Kinney and why did she invite the boys to her home?

4. How did 'Abdu'l-Bahá greet the boys when they arrived?

5. Why did one boy think he might not be welcome?

6. What did 'Abdu'l-Bahá do when that boy entered the room?

7. How did people react to 'Abdu'l-Bahá's announcement, and why?

8. What did 'Abdu'l-Bahá do with the chocolate candy?

9. Without using any words, what did 'Abdu'l-Bahá teach the people in the room?

10. How did 'Abdu'l-Bahá's message affect the young boy?

11. What can we learn from the example of 'Abdu'l-Bahá?

The Power of Unity – Lesson #4

CHOCOLATE ROSES

> *"...Make me a flower of the rose garden..."*
> ('Abdu'l-Bahá, Bahá'í Prayers, p. 36)

Idea from Syndi Duehn

Materials (for each child)

- ☐ Two Hershey's Kisses at room temperature (if too cold, wire won't penetrate)
- ☐ Floral wire, approx. 20 gauge or strong enough to hold the weight of the Kisses. Pre-cut floral wire stems are available in 9-inch (23 cm) lengths.
- ☐ 5 inch (13 cm) squares of red or pink-tinted cellophane
- ☐ Two artificial rose leaves on wire or plastic stems
- ☐ Wire cutters (for cutting off the rose leaves)
- ☐ Floral tape
- ☐ Scissors

Preparation: When working with younger children, pre-cut the cellophane squares. You can use a square cardboard pattern rather than measuring each time. Cut a sufficient number of rose leaves from inexpensive artificial flowers, keeping in mind that longer stems are easier for small children to handle. Cellophane, flowers, floral tape and wire can be found at craft supply, dollar stores and discount department stores.

Instructions

1. Insert the floral wire into the point of one Hershey's Kiss to form the stem. (Tell children not to eat the candy!)

2. Place the two Kisses back to back (flat bottoms together).

3. Cover the top Kiss with cellophane. Then twist the cellophane down around both Kisses to form a rosebud, and continue twisting around the stem.

4. Wrap floral tape tightly around the cellophane at the point where the rosebud meets the stem.

5. Continue wrapping floral tape tightly around the stem, adding the two leaves approximately 1/3 of the way down. Keep wrapping until the wire is completely covered. Gently pull and stretch the tape when winding for a tighter seal.

6. Write your name on a piece of masking tape and wrap it around the stem, since many roses will look alike.

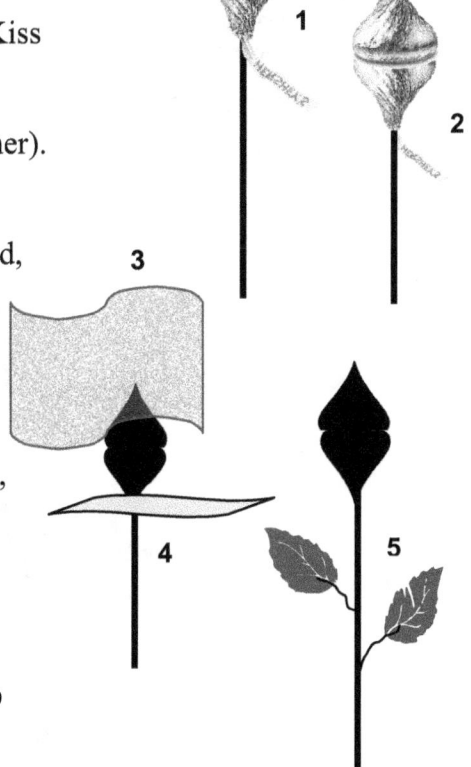

Bahá'í Children's Classes and Retreats: Theme 5, p. 87

The Power of Unity – Lesson #4

"Barriers into Bonds"

Teacher's Guide, Script, and Patterns for Felt Lesson

Adapted from the Star Study Program felt lesson on "The Elimination of Prejudice"
© 1975 by the National Spiritual Assembly of the Bahá'ís of the United States.

TO THE TEACHER: This packet contains a script, instructions, and patterns for making a felt lesson on "Barriers into Bonds." In order to present the lesson, you will need either a felt board or carpet board (see instructions on following pages). A carpet board is more durable and has a more finished look.

After preparing the board, cut out the pattern pieces and stack them in order of use. Read through the script and repeat the actions until you can present the lesson smoothly. Read slowly and clearly, with brief pauses for placement of the felt pieces. The objectives of the lesson are listed below. The children will be able to:

| (1) Describe some of the ways that people are different. | (2) Explain how prejudice has made differences into barriers. | (3) Show how Bahá'u'lláh's teachings can turn barriers into bonds. |

Bahá'í Children's Classes and Retreats: Theme 5, p. 88

The Power of Unity – Lesson #4

Script for Felt Lesson

"Barriers into Bonds"

	NARRATION	ACTION
1	All around the world, people are different in many ways.	Place globe in center of felt board and add the people around it in a circle. 
2	We have different skin colors, speak different languages, come from different cultures, live in different countries, and practice different religions.	As each difference is mentioned, place it above one of the people.
3	Some people dislike others without even knowing them, just because of these differences. This is called prejudice. Because of prejudice, our differences have become barriers between us.	Place the barriers between the people. 
4	But Bahá'u'lláh says that the earth is one country and mankind its citizens.	Indicate the earth and all the people with a circular motion of your hand.
5	When we realize that we all belong to the same human family, we will see our differences as a source of beauty and strength, and these barriers will become bonds of unity.	Flip the barriers over and turn them sideways to form bonds. 
6	When the human family is united, the world will finally be at peace.	Add the dove above the earth. 
7	Bahá'u'lláh says, "The well-being of mankind, its peace and security, are unattainable unless and until its unity is firmly established." *	

* Gleanings, p. 286

The Power of Unity – Lesson #4

Instructions for Making Felt or Carpet Board

A felt board can be purchased at a teacher supply store, or one can be constructed by gluing a large piece of felt onto a stiff backing such as heavy cardboard, thin plywood or masonite. Spray glue gives the best results. A carpet board is constructed in the same way. Felt and glue are available at yardage and craft supply stores.

Materials

- Sharp scissors
- Large piece of felt or indoor-outdoor carpet* (choose beige or other neutral color, approx. 24 x 36 in. or 60 x 90 cm.)
- Backing board (same size as felt or carpet)
- Spray glue or white craft glue

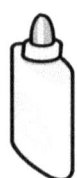

* If using carpet, test a piece of felt to be sure it sticks.
  Some types of carpeting may work better than others.

Instructions for Making Felt Pieces

1. Photocopy the pattern pages.
2. Using the copies, cut around each shape outside the line.
3. Attach each pattern to the appropriate color of felt, using the tape or large paper clip.
4. Carefully cut out each piece, using the pattern as a guide.
5. Cut out the labels and glue to the appropriate felt pieces (see next page).
6. Add velcro as indicated (see next page).
7. Store script and felt pieces in a zip-lock plastic bag for ease of use.

> Pre-cut felt people can also be purchased through teacher supply stores, elementary classroom catalogs, or online at:
> - www.dickblick.com/zz611/47/
> - www.icelebratediversity.com/products/other/crafts/crafts_14.asp
> - www.multiculturalkids.com/Felt-Figures.html

Materials

- Pattern pieces (on following pages)
- Sharp scissors
- Different colors of felt
- Double-stick tape or large paper clip
- Stick-on velcro (plastic loop side)
- White paper to print labels
- White craft glue

The Power of Unity – Lesson #4

Patterns for Felt Lesson on "Barriers into Bonds"

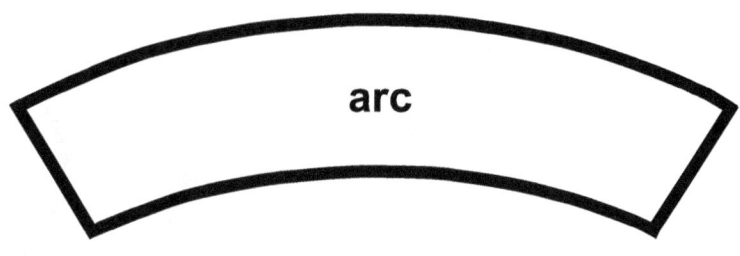

1. Photocopy this page onto cardstock and cut out the arc pattern.

2. Using the **arc** pattern, cut out 5 identical pieces of white felt.

3. Using the same pattern, cut 5 more pieces of felt, each from a different color.

    Use bright colors that contrast with the felt board, for example, red, blue, dark yellow, light green and dark green.

4. Glue each white piece to a colored piece to make 5 felt "sandwiches," and allow to dry.

5. Cut out the 5 paper labels and glue each one onto the white side of a different felt sandwich.

6. Add small pieces of velcro on both sides of each felt sandwich, as indicated below.

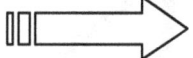

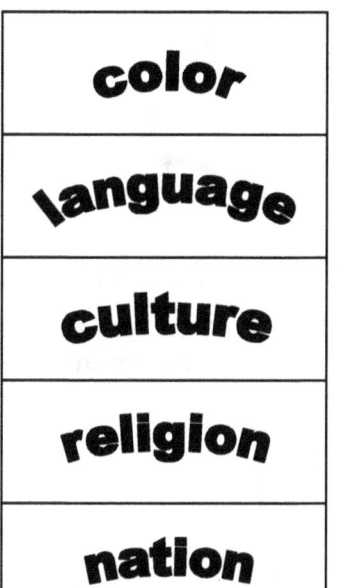

Tip: For easier cut-outs, copy patterns onto peel-and-stick adhesive paper.

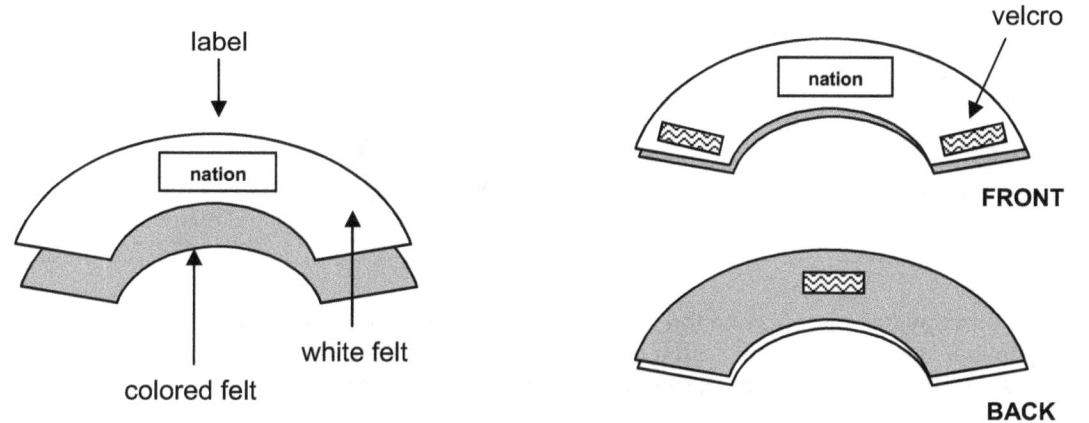

Bahá'í Children's Classes and Retreats: Theme 5, p. 91

The Power of Unity – Lesson #4

Patterns for Felt Lesson on "Barriers into Bonds"

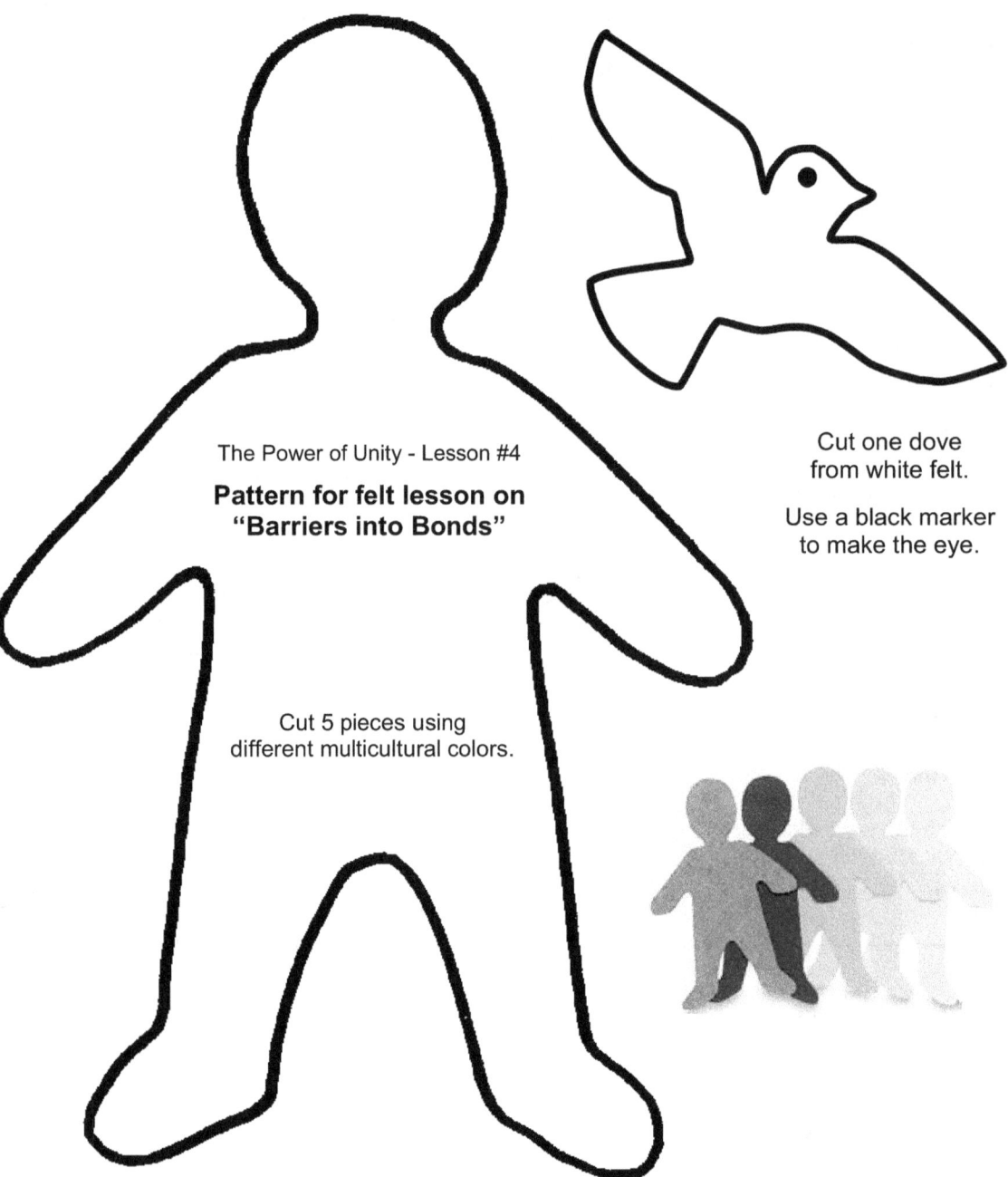

The Power of Unity - Lesson #4

Pattern for felt lesson on "Barriers into Bonds"

Cut 5 pieces using different multicultural colors.

Cut one dove from white felt.

Use a black marker to make the eye.

Photocopy this page. Using the people pattern as a guide, cut out five identical figures, each one from a different color of felt. Use multicultural colors, for example, light brown, dark brown, off-white, copper, pink or beige.

Bahá'í Children's Classes and Retreats: Theme 5, p. 92

The Power of Unity – Lesson #4

Patterns for Felt Lesson on "Barriers into Bonds"

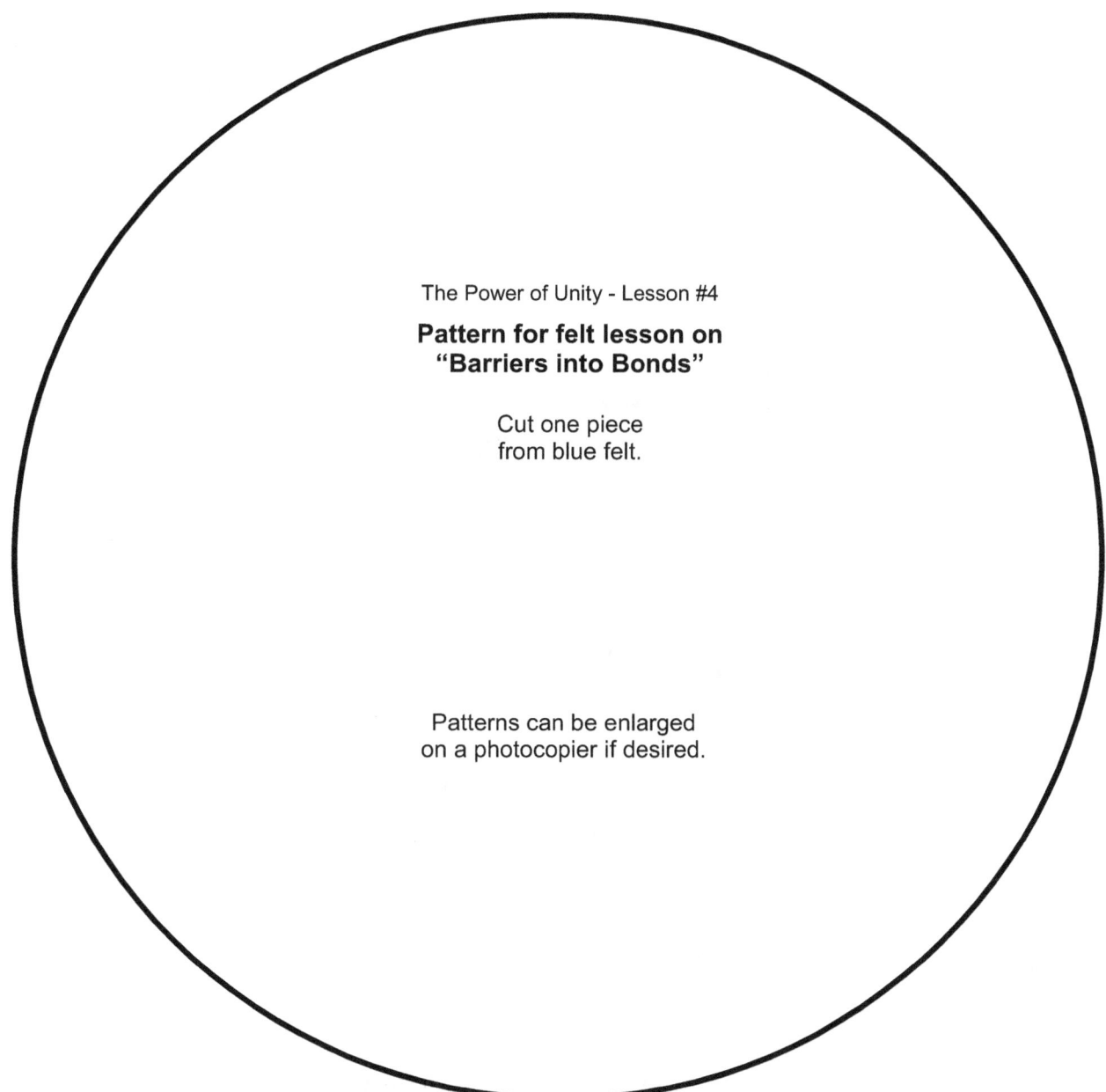

The Power of Unity - Lesson #4

Pattern for felt lesson on "Barriers into Bonds"

Cut one piece from blue felt.

Patterns can be enlarged on a photocopier if desired.

Photocopy this page. Using the pattern as a guide, cut out one blue felt circle to make the earth.

Bahá'í Children's Classes and Retreats: Theme 5, p. 93

The Power of Unity – Lesson #4

Patterns for Felt Lesson on "Barriers into Bonds"

Cut from green felt.

green

Power of Unity - Lesson #4

Pattern for felt lesson on "Barriers into Bonds"

Photocopy this page. Using the patterns as a guide, cut the continents out of green felt and glue them onto the earth as shown below.

Bahá'í Children's Classes and Retreats: Theme 5, p. 94

The Power of Unity – Lesson #4

The Circle of Unity

(Read slowly with feeling.)

We are going to make a unity circle using red yarn. Red is a symbol of the blood of all human beings. We are all part of the circle of life. Each thread represents your special gift—your contribution to the world. As you stand in this circle, quietly tie the ends of your yarn together with your two neighbors, making one knot on the left, and one on the right. This shows that we are all connected. Now take a moment and just quietly honor our circle, as we stand together here.

Now, close your eyes, and without moving, imagine your family and all of your friends joining us here in the circle.

Now enlarge your vision. Add your neighbors to our circle, then your teachers, your soccer coach, your doctor, your church members or Bahá'í community, all the people you know. Imagine everyone smiling. People are welcoming each other. They are happy to be together.

Now invite your entire town into the circle. Without moving, just imagine the circle growing larger and larger. Now include your whole state or province—everyone in the country, and finally, the entire world. Invite every human being into our circle of unity.

Keeping your eyes closed, think of someone you know. Think of one positive thing that you can do to help that person feel part of the circle of humanity. Something that will decrease prejudice and increase unity. Think about what you will do. Remember it. Hold it in your mind and heart and take it with you when you leave here today.

Now, keeping your eyes closed, let's end this class with our first memory quote about unity, from Bahá'u'lláh. All together:

"So powerful is the light of unity that it can illuminate the whole earth."

Good! Now open your eyes.

The Power of Unity – Lesson #4

MATERIALS NEEDED

- ☐ White board, easel, markers, eraser
- ☐ Folders and pens for each student
- ☐ Song sheets and page of quotations for each student [A]
- ☐ Packet of readings and handouts on "The Power of Unity" [A]
    - ☐ Excerpt from *The Sneetches* by Dr. Seuss [B]
    - ☐ "Some Ways to Deal with Putdowns and Prejudice"
    - ☐ "Name It, Claim It, Stop It"
    - ☐ "Creating Unity"
- ☐ Materials for Bridges and Barriers activity:
    - ☐ One red and one green 3x5 index card for each student (or two other colors)
    - ☐ Blank classroom wall or large bulletin board on which to attach the cards
    - ☐ Black markers (one for every two students)
    - ☐ Tape or pushpins
- ☐ Scratch paper and small trash can
- ☐ Additional white board or poster with questions for activity #6
- ☐ "Personal Stories" instructions for group leaders (one copy per volunteer)
- ☐ Felt lesson on "Barriers into Bonds" (script and patterns included)
- ☐ Felt board and easel
- ☐ Reading on "The Circle of Unity" (included)
- ☐ Red yarn cut into 18-inch (46 cm) lengths (one per student)
- ☐ References for teachers (included at the end of this manual)

A. Included in the Handouts section of this teacher's guide.

B. The excerpt from *The Sneetches and Other Stories* is used with permission. The illustrated book (ISBN: 0-394-80089-3) can be ordered from the publisher, Random House Books for Young Readers: <www.randomhouse.com>, or from <www.Amazon.com>. Pictures can be found online at: www.Google.com/images. Type "sneetches" in the search box. If pictures are not available, you can cut out a green five-pointed star to show the children while you read the poem. The complete poem is also online at: <www.barnabasministry.com/quotes-sneeches.html>.

* * * * *

Additional Activities

The Power of Unity

Additional Activities

Warm-ups

1. Birthday line-up 99
2. Link-ups 99
3. Human knot 99

Craft Projects

1. Rainbow chain 100
2. Paper people 100
3. Ribbon of hearts 100
4. Chalk mural 101
5. Leaves of one tree 101-102
6. Pigment posters 103

Outdoor Games

1. Tug of peace 104
2. Cooperative musical chairs 104-105
3. Freeze dance 105
4. Beach ball volley 105
5. Loop-de-hoop 106
6. Lava island 106
7. All aboard 106
8. Fingertip touchdown 107
9. Trust walk 107
10. Electric fence 108
11. Centipede 108

Skits and Demonstrations

1. Colors of the heart 110
2. What's in a name 110
3. Garden flowers 111
4. Cooperation skit 112-113
5. The human body 112, 114-119
6. Seven candles of unity 120-121

Further Reading and Research 122-123

The Power of Unity – Additional Activities

Warm-up Activities

No materials needed

1. BIRTHDAY LINE-UP (5-10 min.)

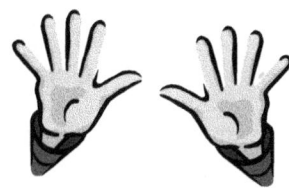

This is a fun activity that requires cooperation in order to succeed.

Tell the children to silently line up in order by age. Youth and adults can play too. There should be no talking or mouthing the words. They can only communicate using gestures. Ask what they would do if several people are the same age. Once the line has been formed, have them check for accuracy by stating their birthdates aloud in turn.

2. LINK-UPS (5-10 min.)

This activity requires group cooperation, helps the children get to know each other better, and highlights some of the things we have in common.

Have the children form a circle with one student (let's call her Keisha) standing in the center. She should say her name and one thing about herself, for example: *"My name is Keisha and I like to ride bikes."*

Another student who also likes to ride bikes, can then link arms with Keisha and say, *"This is Keisha. She likes to ride bikes. My name is Nabil. I also like to ride bikes <u>and</u> I'm wearing blue shorts."*

If another child is wearing blue shorts, he can link arms with Nabil and say, *"This is Nabil. He's wearing blue shorts. My name is Marcus. I'm also wearing blue shorts <u>and</u> I have two sisters."*

If no one else has two sisters, Marcus has to think of something else. In the same way, the remaining students link to the chain, one at a time. The last person must complete the circle by finding something in common with the first person in the chain.

3. HUMAN KNOT (5-10 min.)

This activity requires cooperation, group problem solving and leadership.

- Have all the children stand in a tight circle, shoulder to shoulder.
- Each person grabs the hands of two different people across the circle.
- The goal is for the whole group to untangle itself to form a regular circle, with everyone still holding hands. People can be facing in or out, but they cannot let go. Sometimes the knot unwinds into two or more smaller circles. You can start with smaller groups of 5-10 for an easier experience.

The Power of Unity – Additional Activities

Craft Projects

Display samples of each craft, and allow children to work at their own pace. Completed projects can be used to decorate the facility.

---

1. RAINBOW CHAIN

Materials: Construction paper, ruler, pencils, scissors, glue

 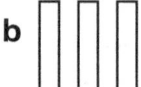

a. Mark construction paper into strips.

b. Cut out strips from different colors of paper.

c. Glue ends of one strip together to form a ring.

d. Repeat with each strip, looping through previous ring before gluing.

---

2. PAPER PEOPLE

Materials: Construction paper, pencils, scissors, glue

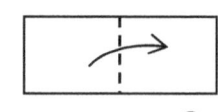 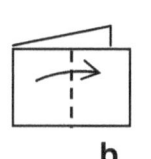 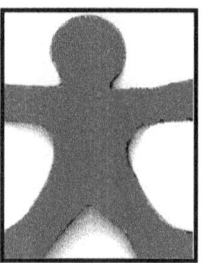

a. Fold long strip of paper in half.

b. Fold in half again.

c. Draw a person with the hands and feet touching both sides.

d. Cut along outline, being careful not to cut through folds at the hands and feet.

e. Unfold the paper, and glue to other people chains.

---

3. RIBBON OF HEARTS

Materials: Construction paper, pencils, scissors, glue, ribbon

Tip: For younger children, the teacher may wish to use heart stencils or make a few heart patterns for tracing.

a. Draw hearts on construction paper.

b. Cut out and glue to ribbon.

The Power of Unity – Additional Activities

4. CHALK MURAL

Materials: Large colored chalk sticks

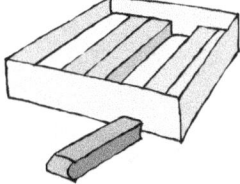

Provide chalk and a driveway, sidewalk or other large cement surface. Invite the children to choose a theme such as "Unity in Diversity" or "We Are One Family," and to paint a cooperative mural. They can work alone or in groups.

5. LEAVES OF ONE TREE

Materials: Construction paper, pencils, leaf patterns, scissors, black marker, masking tape, bare tree branch

a. Trace leaf pattern onto construction paper and cut out.

b. Print your name on leaf with black marker.

c. Tape leaf onto tree.

Preparation

- Obtain a branch from a real tree and strip off all the leaves. (Find one with lots of twigs.)
- Set the branch upright in a large bucket or planter and weight it down with rocks or sand.
- If desired, spray the branch with gold paint and cover the bucket with colorful fabric.
- Set out a tray with ¼-sheets of construction paper in a variety of bright colors.
- Pre-cut several leaf patterns out of cardboard or stiff vinyl for children to trace (next page).
- Add the quote from Bahá'u'lláh (next page, from *Tablets of Bahá'u'lláh*, p. 27).
- These materials can also be set out during the children's performance, and audience members can be invited to add their own leaves to the tree.

"Ye are all the leaves of one tree..."

(Bahá'u'lláh)

Add your name to the tree of humankind.

- -

Copy onto cardstock. Cut on dotted line and post sign next to tree. ↗

The Power of Unity –
Additional Activities

Pattern for "Leaves of One Tree" craft

The Power of Unity –
Additional Activities

Pattern for "Leaves of One Tree" craft

Make several copes of each leaf pattern out of cardboard or stiff vinyl for children to trace.

Bahá'í Children's Classes and Retreats: Theme 5, p. 102

6. PIGMENT POSTERS

Materials: Poster board, pencils, rulers, scissors, glue sticks, and construction paper or paint sample strips in multicultural colors

Multicultural construction paper can be found at craft and teacher-supply stores. It can also be ordered through many online sites, including: *www.dickblick.com/products/pacon-multicultural-construction-paper*. Paint samples can be found at paint and hardware stores.

Instructions

a. Cut the construction paper or paint color strips into a variety of shapes.
b. Glue the shapes onto the poster board to form an abstract design.
c. If desired, include a quote from the Bahá'í Writings (see samples below) or add your own thoughts about the beauty of our diverse skin tones.
d. Write your name on the back of the poster.

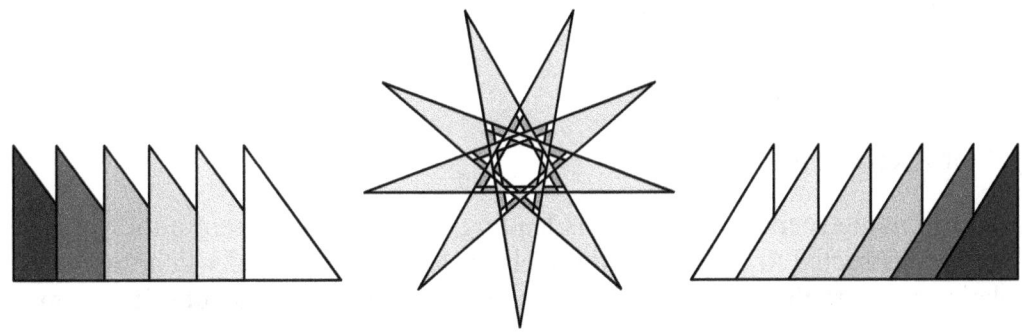

"Bahá'u'lláh hath said that the various races of humankind lend a composite harmony and beauty of color to the whole..." ('Abdu'l-Bahá, *Promulgation of Universal Peace*, p. 68)

"...this difference and this variation...are the cause of the appearance of beauty and perfection." ('Abdu'l-Bahá, *Tablet to the Hague*, p. 14)

"Nay, rather, the very fact that there is difference and variety lends a charm to the garden." ('Abdu'l-Bahá, *Foundations of World Unity*, p. 34)

"Even though each soul has its own individual perfume and color, all are reflecting the same light..." ('Abdu'l-Bahá, *Promulgation of Universal Peace*, p. 24)

The Power of Unity – Additional Activities

Outdoor Games

The following activities are fun, easy to organize, require few materials, and relate to the theme of unity. Prizes can be provided after the games. Allow at least 20 minutes for each activity.*

1. TUG OF PEACE

Materials: Sturdy rope

Form a circle with a length of sturdy rope that has been tied in a knot. Have the children stand equally-spaced around the circle and squat down, while holding onto the rope with both hands. At the count of three, the children should lean back while pulling on the rope, and slowly stand up together. When everyone is up, you can count to three again, and have them carefully lean back and squat down. A smaller circle of rope makes it easier.

This game contrasts with the typical tug-of-war in which players pit their strength against one another, beating their opponents by dragging them through the mud. Tug of Peace serves as a graphic demonstration of cooperation and mutual support, and makes it obvious to the children that they are able to achieve something together that they could not do alone.

2. COOPERATIVE MUSICAL CHAIRS

Materials: Sturdy chairs, lively music

Consider the following scenario. An adult is leading a group of children in the game of musical chairs. They are instructed to walk around the chairs to the music, and when the music stops, to sit in the chair nearest to them. The child who is left without a chair is out of the game.

The children do as they are told, circling around the chairs and eyeing each other with nervous suspicion. When the music stops, they scramble for a seat, knocking each other over and shoving others out of the way. If two children try to sit on the same chair, the stronger one pushes the weaker one onto the floor.

The child who is eliminated goes over to the corner to cry. A well-meaning adult approaches and says, "It's just a game. You're not being a very good sport." The chairs are removed, one by one, and when the game is over, only one child is victorious—the last one left with a chair. Aggressive behavior has been rewarded, and the teacher asks, "Now wasn't that fun?"

What do students learn from playing this game? They learn that there are not enough chairs to go around; that pushing and shoving in the name of "winning" are acceptable behaviors; and that it's okay to shove a child who is smaller or weaker, or who doesn't understand the game. They learn to use people's differences against them in order to win. This kind of competition is destructive to community.

* The first two games were adapted from *Because We Can Change the World* by Mara Sapon-Shevin.
Games 6-10 adapted from: < www.usscouts.org/usscouts/games > and < www.group-games.com >.

We could play, instead, **Cooperative Musical Chairs**. In this version of the game, children walk around the chairs to the music, and although there are fewer chairs than children, the goal is that everyone must be on a chair for the group to win. (If chairs are not available, you can use carpet squares or pieces of construction paper instead.) Remove one chair before the music starts each time. The game ends when there is one chair left for every 4-5 children.

What happens? The children share chairs, they sit on laps, they laugh. The goal is not to exclude, but as a group, to figure out how everyone can be included. As the number of chairs is reduced, the challenge increases, and the children must engage in problem solving and negotiation to achieve the goal. For safety, chairs must be sturdy enough to hold the weight of several children without collapsing. Adult safety monitors are recommended.

3. FREEZE DANCE

Materials: A small object for each child, lively music

This activity is designed to teach cooperation and helpfulness. Unlike most games where the object is to eliminate others, the goal of Freeze Dance is to make sure everyone is included. It can be played by any size group, of various ages and levels of mobility.

The participants each place a small object on their heads (e.g., a knotted sock, toy animal, paper plate or bean bag), and begin to dance while lively music is played in the background.

If someone's bean bag falls off, that person must freeze until another player notices and replaces the bean bag without losing their own. If the helper's bean bag falls off, the helper is also frozen until someone else comes to the rescue. Keep playing as long as everyone is having fun, or until the music runs out!

4. BEACH BALL VOLLEY

Materials: Inflated beach ball or large balloon

Have children form a circle, arm's length apart. Give them the ball to volley, and have them practice gently popping it up a few times. Then challenge them to keep it in the air for 10 hits, then 20, etc. Encourage them to develop strategies, such as passing the ball around the circle or putting someone in the middle.

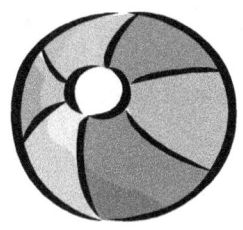

The Power of Unity – Additional Activities

5. LOOP-DE-HOOP

Materials: Hula hoops of different sizes

Have the children stand in a circle holding hands. Start with a hula hoop (or bike inner tube) hanging over one pair of joined hands. Each person in the circle must pass the hoop over him/herself and on to the next person without letting go of their hands. For an added challenge, try this with two or three hoops of different sizes, going in different directions at the same time.

6. LAVA ISLAND

Materials: Rope, small object for each child

In a relatively clean flat area, form a circle on the ground with the rope. The circle should be large enough to hold all the children and allow them room to work. Each child should have a small object (e.g., a paper cup, scarf or water bottle).

Have the children space themselves evenly around the outside of the circle. Tell them to sit on the ground with their legs straight, feet touching the perimeter. Next, have them place their cups just behind them on the ground. Then have them get up and stand inside the circle.

Explain that they are now surrounded by a pool of hot lava. The only safe spot is the "island" they are now standing on (marked by the circle you created). The goal is to bring all the cups onto the island without touching the lava (anything outside the circle) and without using anything other than themselves (no hats, sticks, etc.). The solution involves hanging onto one person as he/she leans out and grabs the cup. In doing so, the person's body will be nearly parallel to the ground.

This is a great team-building game, and can be played by several groups at once, or by the class as a whole.

7. ALL ABOARD!

Materials: Tarp or old sheet

This game is similar to Cooperative Musical Chairs. Start with something foldable and not too slippery (e.g. a tarp) to represent a train. Spread the tarp on the ground and explain that when "All aboard!" is called, everyone must stand on the train without touching the ground. Try it once to be sure everyone understands the directions. Then say, "Now, everyone <u>off</u> the train!"

Next, fold the tarp in half. Lay it back on the ground and call "All aboard!" once again. The children must cooperate in order for everyone to ride the train. Keep folding the tarp in half until it's too small to continue.

With a large group, break into smaller teams of 5-10, making them roughly equal in the number and size of the children. Strategies include standing on one leg and riding piggyback. Safety monitors are recommended.

8. FINGERTIP TOUCHDOWN

Materials: One hula hoop for every 3-4 children

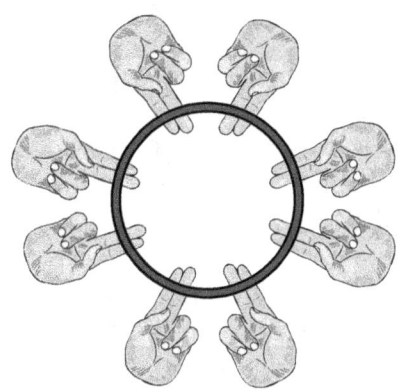

This activity requires concentration and teamwork. Divide the class into small groups and give each group a hula hoop. The children should stand in a circle around their hoop, holding it from underneath with two fingertips from each hand. On the count of three, have them lower the hoop to the ground, and raise it back up again, without anyone's fingertips losing contact. It's harder than it looks!

For an additional challenge, have them try it again without talking, or add more people to each hoop, or see how many touchdowns each team can make in one minute.

9. TRUST WALK

Materials: Blindfolds for half the children, flags or cones to mark start and finish lines, obstacles

This activity teaches trust, cooperation and communication. It requires a large safe open space, and a variety of large and small objects to serve as obstacles (hay bales, cardboard boxes, water balloons, rolled up socks, Frisbees, plastic wading pools, rubber snakes, ropes, etc.), but nothing sharp or dangerous.

Mark start and finish lines for the game area and set out the obstacles. More obstacles make for a more challenging course. Station a few volunteers around the field for safety.

Begin the game by having everyone form pairs at the starting line. Spread them out to avoid collisions on the field. One partner will be blindfolded and the other will be the guide. Explain that the guides are responsible for their partner's safety. When everyone is ready, have the guides slowly spin their blindfolded partners around so they lose their sense of direction.

From this point on, the guides should not touch their partners at all, but can use verbal cues to talk them through the obstacle course without touching anything, e.g., "In three more steps, there will be a water balloon. Step over it slowly."

Anyone who touches an obstacle must return to the starting line. (Guides can hold their partners hands when bringing them back, or blindfolds can be removed to allow for a speedier return.) When all have reached the finish line, have the partners switch roles so everyone has a turn.

Reflection: After the activity, you can ask the children what they learned from the experience. Some sample questions:

- What do you think was the purpose of this activity?
- What was it like to be blindfolded?
- What was it like to be the guide?
- How did it feel when you trusted each other and worked together to accomplish something challenging?

10. ELECTRIC FENCE

Materials: Rope, two posts or someone to hold the rope on each end

Tie a rope between two trees or posts and have the children gather on one side. The rope should be high enough so no one can step over it. Tell the group that this is an electric fence—the fence of prejudice, and anyone touching it will get a nasty shock.

The goal is to pass everyone safely over the fence, one by one. If someone touches the fence, the entire group must start over. Set a few ground rules (e.g., no crawling under the fence or diving over it, and it's okay to take off your shoes). Then ask the children to consult together to figure out how to reach the other side. They should make a plan before they begin.

11. CENTIPEDE

Materials: Scarf, old necktie or rope for each child; flags or cones to mark start and finish lines

In the traditional version of this game, the three-legged race, two partners with their inside legs tied together, compete against other teams in a short running race. They must cooperate in order to run together without falling.

In this new version of the game, all the children stand shoulder to shoulder along the starting line. Volunteers then help them tie their legs together at the ankles, with the left leg of each child strapped to the right leg of the next child in line. Each tie should be long enough to make a bow. Be sure it isn't too tight and that nothing is hanging down to trip up the team.

Rather than competing against each other, the goal is for everyone to make it safely to the finish line together. It will take teamwork to make this centipede walk! For an added challenge, you can time the "race." Safety monitors are recommended.

The Power of Unity – Additional Activities

Outdoor Games

Bahá'í Children's Classes and Retreats: Theme 5, p. 109

The Power of Unity – Additional Activities

Skits and Demonstrations

These short skits and demonstrations are intended to reinforce the concepts presented during class. They can be included as part of the children's final performance if desired.

1. COLORS OF THE HEART

Materials

- ❏ M&M candies
- ❏ One bowl for each color of M&M
- ❏ Several blindfolds

Instructions

Assign roles (1 teacher and several students) and act out the following situation:

1. The teacher asks the students to sort M&Ms into the bowls by color.
2. The students are then blindfolded and asked to determine which color tastes best.
3. After sampling a few, the students protest that they all taste the same, but the teacher insists that they must choose one.
4. Students repeat the taste test, then remove the blindfolds and explain that while M&Ms look different on the outside, inside they're all chocolate!
5. Teacher then explains that people are like that too: different on the outside, but inside we're all human beings. What's important is not the color of the skin, but the heart.

If desired, the children can memorize one of the following quotations to recite at the end of the skit (#14 and #18 on their quotations page).

#14. *"God does not look at colors; He looks at the hearts."*
('Abdu'l-Bahá, Promulgation of Universal Peace, p. 44)

#18. *"Close your eyes to racial differences, and welcome all with the light of oneness."*
(Bahá'u'lláh, quoted in Shoghi Effendi, Advent of Divine Justice, p. 37)

2. WHAT'S IN A NAME?

This activity takes some thought, and makes a good homework assignment. Tell students to use the letters of their first name to create a statement relating to one of the topics they have studied in class (see examples below). They can recite their statements for the children's performance.

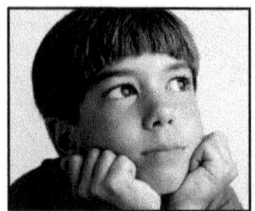

R = Racial	D = Diversity	M = Mankind
A = Amity	I = Is	A = Actually
N = Not	A = Always	N = Needs
D = Division	N = Nice	U = Unity &
I = In	E = Everywhere	E = Extra
E = Every heart		L = Love

Bahá'í Children's Classes and Retreats: Theme 5, p. 110

3. GARDEN FLOWERS

Materials

- ❏ Crayons or colored pencils
- ❏ Drawing paper

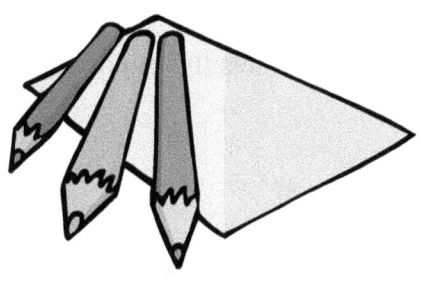

Instructions

Assign parts (one teacher, several students) and have the children role play the following scene using their own words.

	Teacher	Students
1	Children, I'd like you each to choose a pencil or crayon of your favorite color.	My favorite is blue! I like green! (Etc.)
2	Good! Now draw a picture of a flower garden using only your favorite color.	Students work on their drawings.*
3	Hold up your work and let's see what you've done.	Students hold up their drawings.
4	Nice job! Now draw a second picture of the flower garden, this time using lots of different colors.	Students work on their second drawing.
5	Hold up both of your pictures side by side. Which one was more fun to draw? Which one do you like best? Why?	Students hold up both pictures and share their thoughts.
6	Yes, diversity adds beauty and makes the flower garden more interesting!	Have one or more students recite quote #10 (below).

* You may wish to have the children prepare their drawings in advance, and pretend to color during the performance, in order to save time.

> *"Behold a beautiful garden full of flowers...Each flower has a different charm, a peculiar beauty, its own delicious perfume and beautiful colour... It is just the diversity and variety that constitutes its charm..."* ('Abdu'l-Bahá, Paris Talks, p. 52)

The Power of Unity – Additional Activities

4. COOPERATION SKIT

This humorous skit demonstrates the importance of working together in unity.

Materials

- ❏ White board with marker
- ❏ Eleven students
- ❏ Poster board to make eleven large cards that spell out the word "cooperation"
  (A note to each student should be taped on the back of the cards—see next page.)

Instructions

1. Write the word "COOPERATION" on the board.
2. Give each student one of the cards.
3. Ask them to silently read the note on the back of the card, but not to share this with anyone.*
4. Then tell them to try to spell "COOPERATION" by lining up in order as quickly as possible, while acting out the directions on their card. *(If they follow the directions, they will not be able to spell the word.)*
5. Allow the skit to run for a minute, then call, "Stop!"
6. Tell the students to try again, but this time, they should really cooperate.
   (It should be a lot easier the second time around.)

* When performing this skit for an audience, omit step #3 (or at least don't say it out loud). The students will have already practiced this, and will know to make it difficult the first time.

<u>Tip:</u> For a smaller class, you can do a similar skit with only five students. Have them spell the word "U-N-I-T-Y." (See next page for sample notes to tape on each card.) On the second try, students should be able to spell the word with no trouble. Close by having one student explain that we can reach UNITY by putting "U" before "I" ("you" before "I").

5. FELT LESSON: "The Human Body"

Present the felt lesson on "The Human Body" (see patterns and instructions on page 114 following the "Cooperation" script below). Then ask if some of the students would like to present it without your help in front of the class or to volunteer for the children's performance.

The Power of Unity – Additional Activities

Photocopy this page, cut into rows, and tape to the back of the appropriate card for activity #4.

C	Complain about everyone else.
O	Fight with the other "O"s over who should go first.
O	Fight with the other "O"s over who should go first.
P	Push people out of your way.
E	Try to line up on either end. Refuse to be in the middle.
R	Repeat the same thing over and over.
A	Argue that "A" is the first letter of the alphabet and should go first.
T	Tell everyone else how to line up.
I	Insist that "I" is the most important letter.
O	Fight with the other "O"s over who should go first.
N	Take a nap.

U	Push others out of your way, since "you" are first.
N	Take a nap.
I	Insist that "I" is the most important letter and should go first.
T	Tell everyone else how to line up.
Y	Complain about everyone else. Yak, yak, yak!

The Power of Unity – Additional Activities

"The Human Body"

Teacher's Guide, Script, and Patterns for Felt Lesson

TO THE TEACHER: This packet contains a script, instructions, and patterns for making a felt lesson on "The Human Body." The lesson demonstrates the importance of unity in diversity, and the debilitating effects of prejudice. It builds on a previous felt lesson about "The Eye" from class #2.

You will need the felt board or carpet board prepared earlier (see instructions on page 43). After cutting out the pattern pieces, read through the script and repeat the actions until you can present the lesson smoothly. The objectives of the lesson are listed below. The children will be able to:

(1) Depict the human body as a concrete example of unity in diversity.

(2) Describe the negative effects of prejudice and discrimination.

(3) Explain the value of diversity and the need for unity.

The Power of Unity – Additional Activities

Script for Felt Lesson

"The Human Body"

	NARRATION	ACTION
1	**Consider the human body.** It begins as a single cell, which grows and develops into the various tissues, organs and limbs.	Place cell on board. Cover cell with body.
2	Each part has an important role: • The heart pumps our blood… • The lungs enable us to breathe… • And the eyes allow us to see.	• Add heart. • Breathe in and out. • Add eyes.
3	If all the parts are strong, the body functions well.	Add smile.
4	Any part (a heart, a lung, an eye) is useless by itself. It only has value when it works together with the rest of the body.	Hold up the heart. Put heart back on body.
5	• If one part is weak or missing, • the entire body is handicapped. • Or dead!	• Remove one leg. • Change smile to a frown. • Remove heart.
6	**The human race is like the human body.** Like the body's parts, people have different abilities, and come in different shapes and colors. But together we are one human race.	Add leg and heart. Change frown to a smile.
7	Our diversity is our strength. No one group or person can do it alone. We need the contributions of each and all.	Hold up one eye, then replace it.
8	Including women and girls. Without their contributions, half of the body of humanity wouldn't function. We need all the parts of our human family to be healthy and strong.	Cover half of the body with your hand or a piece of paper, then uncover it.
9	**Prejudice is like a cancer,** eating away at the heart of humanity. Discrimination against even one group hurts us all.	Replace good heart with bad one, and change smile to frown.
10	**The Bahá'í Faith teaches** that if we meet those who are different from ourselves, we should "think of them as different coloured roses growing in the beautiful garden of humanity, and rejoice to be among them."*	End with the good heart and a smile.

*'Abdu'l-Bahá, Paris Talks, p. 53

The Power of Unity – Additional Activities

Felt Lesson on The Human Body

Instructions for Making Felt Pieces

1. Photocopy the pattern pages.
2. Using the copies, cut around each shape outside the line.
3. Attach each pattern to the appropriate color of felt using the tape or large paper clips.
4. Carefully cut out each piece, using the pattern as a guide.
5. Glue cell nucleus to cell body and allow to dry.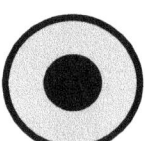
6. Add velcro as indicated (see instructions on pattern pages).
7. Store script and felt pieces in a zip-lock plastic bag for ease of use.

Materials

- ❑ Different colors of felt (see chart below)
- ❑ Pattern pieces (on following pages)
- ❑ Sharp scissors
- ❑ Double-stick tape or large paper clips
- ❑ Stick-on velcro (plastic loop side)
- ❑ White craft glue

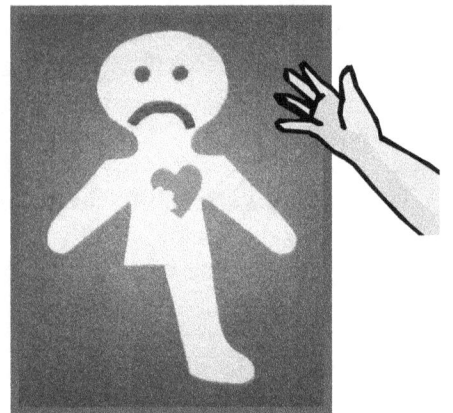

ITEM	COLOR
Cell body	Light orange
Cell nucleus	Black
Human body	Light brown
Heart	Red
Eyes	Dark blue
Mouth	Black

References from Shoghi Effendi

1. "…the virus of prejudice and corruption is eating into the vitals* of an already gravely disordered society." (*Promised Day Is Come,* p. 16)

2. "…a fraternity freed from that cancerous growth of racial prejudice, which is eating into the vitals of an already debilitated society…" (*Advent of Divine Justice,* p. 22)

3. "As to racial prejudice, the corrosion of which, for well-nigh a century, has bitten into the fiber and attacked the whole social structure of American society…" (*Advent of Divine Justice,* p. 33)

* **Vitals:** The body's essential organs, necessary to maintain life.

The Power of Unity – Additional Activities

Patterns for Felt Lesson on "The Human Body"

Cut one heart from red felt.

Pattern for Felt Lesson on "The Human Body"

BCR Theme 5 – Additional Activities

(Join pattern to bottom half of body on next page, then cut figure from light brown felt.)

Cut one heart from red felt.

Patterns can be enlarged on photocopier if desired.

Bahá'í Children's Classes and Retreats: Theme 5, p. 117

The Power of Unity – Additional Activities

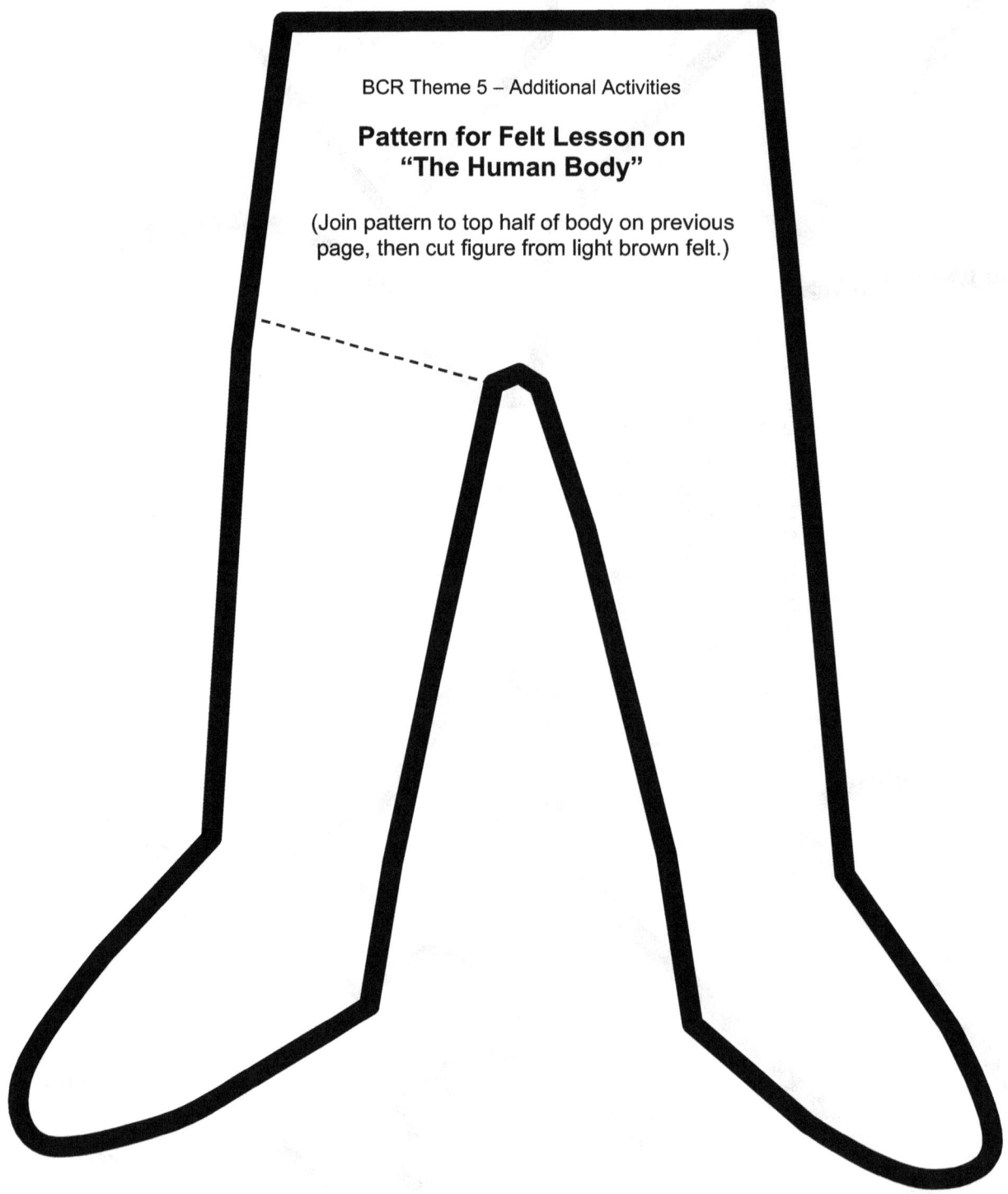

BCR Theme 5 – Additional Activities

Pattern for Felt Lesson on "The Human Body"

(Join pattern to top half of body on previous page, then cut figure from light brown felt.)

The Power of Unity – Additional Activities

Tape together patterns for top and bottom of body, then cut whole body from one piece of felt.

Cut off one leg from body as indicated.

Cut two eyes from dark blue felt.

Cut cell nucleus from black felt, then glue to cell body.

Cut cell body from light orange or yellow felt.

← Cut mouth from black felt.

If necessary, add velcro to the back of each piece so it sticks to the felt board. Small felt pieces may stick easily without velcro.

BACK

Bahá'í Children's Classes and Retreats: Theme 5, p. 119

The Power of Unity – Additional Activities

6. SEVEN CANDLES OF UNITY

This is a dramatic reading of 'Abdu'l-Bahá's prophecy about the unity of humankind. The activity is also described in *Bahá'í Public Speaking* (p. 117).

Materials

- ❑ A copy of the entire passage for each student (see next page)
- ❑ Additional copies of the passage to distribute to the audience (optional)
- ❑ Highlighter pen
- ❑ Candles, candleholders, matches or lighter
- ❑ Metal spoon or candle snuffer*
- ❑ Soft background music (optional)
- ❑ Globe or photo of the earth (optional)
- ❑ Small table to hold the globe and the candles

  * **Snuffer:** A small metal cup used to extinguish candles without blowing wax on the table

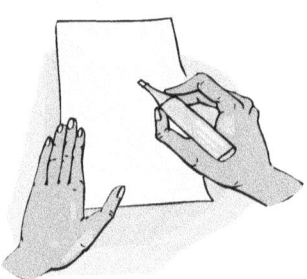

Instructions

1. Divide the passage into parts and select one reader for each part.
2. Give each reader a copy of the entire passage with her or his part highlighted.
3. Discuss the meaning of each sentence and help children pronounce unfamiliar words.
4. Encourage children to memorize their parts and to speak with a strong clear voice.
5. Practice with all of the children lined up in order in front of the room.
6. Rehearse together several times and practice with a microphone if one will be used.
7. Have the readers light each candle as it is mentioned in the second paragraph.
8. For the performance, have students wear ethnic clothing from around the world.
9. If possible, choose a room with lights on a dimmer switch so they can be turned down at the appropriate moment ("…the world's darkened horizon").
10. Sit in the front row with the script to prompt students in case they forget a line.
11. Extinguish candles after the presentation.

SEVEN CANDLES OF UNITY

Selections from the Writings of 'Abdu'l-Bahá, p. 31-33

In cycles gone by, though harmony was established, yet, owing to the absence of means, the unity of all mankind could not have been achieved. Continents remained widely divided, nay even among the peoples of one and the same continent association and interchange of thought were well nigh impossible. Consequently intercourse, understanding and unity amongst all the peoples and kindreds of the earth were unattainable. In this day, however, means of communication have multiplied, and the five continents of the earth have virtually merged into one....In like manner all the members of the human family, whether peoples or governments, cities or villages, have become increasingly interdependent. For none is self-sufficiency any longer possible, inasmuch as political ties unite all peoples and nations, and the bonds of trade and industry, of agriculture and education, are being strengthened every day. Hence the unity of all mankind can in this day be achieved. Verily this is none other but one of the wonders of this wondrous age, this glorious century. Of this past ages have been deprived, for this century – the century of light – hath been endowed with unique and unprecedented glory, power and illumination. Hence the miraculous unfolding of a fresh marvel every day. Eventually it will be seen how bright its candles will burn in the assemblage of man.

Behold how its light is now dawning upon the world's darkened horizon. The first candle is unity in the political realm, the early glimmerings of which can now be discerned. The second candle is unity of thought in world undertakings, the consummation of which will erelong be witnessed. The third candle is unity in freedom which will surely come to pass. The fourth candle is unity in religion which is the corner-stone of the foundation itself, and which, by the power of God, will be revealed in all its splendour. The fifth candle is the unity of nations – a unity which in this century will be securely established, causing all the peoples of the world to regard themselves as citizens of one common fatherland. The sixth candle is unity of races, making of all that dwell on earth peoples and kindreds of one race. The seventh candle is unity of language, i.e., the choice of a universal tongue in which all peoples will be instructed and converse. Each and every one of these will inevitably come to pass, inasmuch as the power of the Kingdom of God will aid and assist in their realization.

Further Reading and Research

Some students may be interested in exploring the themes presented in more detail. Below is a small sampling of books for further reading and research. The stories can also be read to the class, or one or more students might put together a book report to share with their peers.

1. **"People"** by Peter Spier, 1988.
   ISBN-10: 038524469X and ISBN-13: 978-0385244695
   Also available in Spanish from www.Amazon.com
   (enter *gente* and *spier* in the search box).

   In this encyclopedic picture book, the author celebrates human similarities and differences, in what we wear, how we eat, speak, worship and play. This book portrays something of the amazing variety of human life on Earth. Suitable for all ages.

2. **"I Love My Hair"** by Natasha Anastasia Tarpley, 1998.
   ISBN: 9780316522755

   Every night before she goes to bed, Keyana sits down between her mother's knees to have her hair combed. Keyana doesn't feel lucky to have such a head of hair—until Mama reminds her of all the lovely ways her wonderful hair can be fixed. The beautiful watercolor illustrations move from the intimacy of Keyana's bedroom to the neighborhood streets and finally to the whole world

3. **"Two Mrs. Gibsons"** by Toyomi Igus, 2001.
   ISBN: 9780892391707

   There are two Mrs. Gibsons in this young girl's life and she remembers both of them with love. The older Mrs. Gibson has skin the color of chocolate, big hands and a big voice, and she gives big, fat hugs. The younger Mrs. Gibson has skin the color of vanilla, writes Japanese, and cooks Japanese dishes. It is not until the end of the book that readers discover that the first Mrs. Gibson is the girl's grandmother, while the second Mrs. Gibson is her mother.

4. **"Black Is Brown Is Tan"** by Arnold Adoff
   and Emily Arnold Mccully, 1973 and 2004.
   ISBN: 9780064432696 and ISBN-10: 0064436446

   Now a classic, this is a beloved story of an African-American mother, a white father, and their two "tan" children in a loving extended family. Softly-colored pictures with poetic, rhyming text sing the joys of family life and appreciate the many skin tones in their bi-racial family. The language is as magical as the message.

The Power of Unity – Additional Activities

5. **"Stephen Biesty's Incredible Body"** by Stephen Biesty and Richard Platt, 1998.
   ISBN 10: 0789434245 / 0-7894-3424-5
   ISBN 13: 9780789434241

   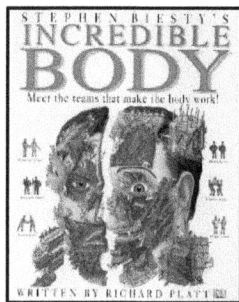

   A fascinating journey through the inner workings of the human body, this oversized volume features cross-sectional illustrations of various organs and systems. Young readers are taken on a tour of the eye, brain, spinal cord, muscles, mouth and gut. The detailed pen-and-ink color drawings are remarkable, and the book can serve to deepen children's understanding of the concept of unity in diversity.

For More Children's Literature and Ideas for Teachers

Awesome Library: Extensive list of multicultural links on various topics, including specific ethnic groups, countries, languages, holidays and religious faiths. < *www.awesomelibrary.org/ Classroom/Social_Studies/Multicultural/Multicultural.html*

Teaching for Change: Dedicated to helping students and teachers build a more equitable society and become active global citizens, this organization offers an annotated list of multicultural literature for children on the theme of "Learning about Racial Identity and Fairness." < *http://teachingforchange.org/publications/abe/racialidentity* >

Teaching Tolerance: A wealth of free anti-bias materials, teaching kits, videos, classroom activities and professional development resources. < *www.tolerance.org* >

Understanding Prejudice: Interactive exercises, searchable databases and over 2,000 links on prejudice, stereotyping and discrimination. < *www.understandingprejudice.org* >

Children's Performance

The Power of Unity

CHILDREN'S PERFORMANCE*

To the Coordinator

The children's performance provides the students an opportunity to demonstrate and reinforce what they have learned. This is often the highlight for children and adults. The fact that children will be performing in front of a live audience serves as excellent motivation for them to learn the material presented in class. The program includes prayers, songs, memorized passages, short talks, demonstrations to illustrate various concepts, a showing of crafts, a poem, skit and mini-opera. The following pages include a detailed agenda for the event, rehearsal instructions, scripts and other materials. Feel free to modify the program to suit the needs of the participants.

As the coordinator, it will be helpful for you to sit in on classes and take notes on which children might be best suited for which type of presentation. Some will memorize quotes easily, others may be good at explaining a concept, and still others might enjoy acting or saying a prayer. Assign parts or ask for volunteers. Be sure everyone is included.

One or two children should be asked to serve as Master or Mistress of Ceremonies (MC). Select children who are responsible, with strong voices and stage presence, who can keep the program moving forward. This places the children center stage and in charge of the presentation.

Before the rehearsal, gather any props and costumes, and remind the adult and youth volunteers that you will need their assistance. Determine their preferences for rehearsal groups. A copy of the agenda and the rehearsal groups should be given to each volunteer. Copies of the appropriate script or reading should be given to the adults and children who will be working on that part of the program.

Rehearsal for the Show

During rehearsal time, the coordinator's tasks include:

- ❑ Meet together with all the participants to explain the nature of the program.
- ❑ Talk about program order, where to sit, use of strong voices so the audience can hear, eye contact, learning the parts rather than reading them, and how to use a microphone if needed.
- ❑ Assign adults and youth to work with each rehearsal group.
- ❑ Assign parts to each child depending on interest and ability.
- ❑ Distribute costumes and props as appropriate.
- ❑ Inform groups when the rehearsal time is almost over.
- ❑ Collect all props and set them out for the show.

> * Note: While the children's performance has typically been scheduled for the evening, the program could be held at any time. During a weekend retreat, Saturday evening is often the most convenient time for inviting neighbors and friends. This means that activities from the fourth class on Sunday morning will not be included in the presentation. If using a weekly format, however, these activities can easily be added to the final program.

The Power of Unity – Children's Performance

MATERIALS NEEDED

Note: Items in italics are included with this section.

- *Agenda*
- *Rehearsal groups* and *Rehearsal notes*
- Welcome sign (if desired)
- *Sample program* (for distributing to the audience)
- Background music (to be played as people are arriving)
- Microphone and sound system (if needed)
- Art exhibit (children's art can be hung from a clothesline or displayed on the wall)
- Song sheets for all (including audience) and music (for song leader)
- Felt board and easel
- *Opening prayer* ("Unite the hearts…")
- Memory quotes
- Stick and bundle of sticks for skit
- Sturdy chair for skit
- *The Eye* (script and felt pieces)
- *Hooray for Skin* (poem)
- Colors of Our World (four color pictures)
- *How We Got Our Skin Color* (script and props for skit)
- *Barriers into Bonds* (script and felt pieces)
- *We Can Build a Beautiful World* (song sheet and costumes for mini-opera)
- Craft samples
    __ Flowers of One Garden (poster)
    __ Chocolate Rose
    __ Leaf Laminate
    __ Diversity Streamer
    __ Personal Poster
- Refreshments

Note: If the children's performance is done after Lesson #4, you can include a short talk on prejudice, the Sneetches poem, a few role plays on responding to prejudice, the additional memory quote, the song "What Mankind Has to Learn," and other activities from that lesson. You can also include the craft projects, skits and demonstrations from the "Additional Activities" section if desired.

The Power of Unity – Children's Performance

 **SAMPLE AGENDA FOR MC (90 min.)**

(1) **Welcome guests** to our program on **"THE POWER OF UNITY"** (cell phones off)

(2) **Opening Music** _____ **Prayer** ("Unite the hearts…") _____

(3) **Intro** (don't read): There is only one race of people in the world, the human race. We come in different shapes, sizes and colors, but we are one human family. We live on one planet and we are children of one God—who wants us to live in peace. In order to have peace, Bahá'u'lláh says we must first have unity. We have been studying about unity all weekend, and tonight we are pleased to present what we have learned.

(4) **Introduce** each section and each presenter and thank them afterwards.

THE POWER OF UNITY (15 min.)
- ❏ Song: We Are Drops (ALL)
- ❏ **Say**: Unity is one of the most important teachings of Bahá'u'lláh, the Founder of the Bahá'í Faith. These next two skits will help us understand why unity is so important.
- ❏ Stick and bundle demo _____
- ❏ Heavy chair skit _____
- ❏ Memory quote: "So powerful…" _____
- ❏ Memory quote: "The well-being of mankind…" _____

UNITY IN DIVERSITY (20 min.)
- ❏ Song: Si Estamos Juntos (ALL)
- ❏ Memory quote: "Regard ye not…" _____
- ❏ Short talk on Unity in Diversity _____
- ❏ Crafts: Flowers of One Garden (poster) _____ and Leaf Laminate _____
- ❏ Musical demo: Row Your Boat _____
- ❏ Felt lesson: The Eye _____
- ❏ Song: One Planet, One People (ALL)

THE COLORS WE ARE (20 min.)
- ❏ Poem: Hooray for Skin _____
- ❏ Craft: Personal poster _____
- ❏ Memory quote: "God does not look at colors…" _____
- ❏ Song: Good Neighbors (ALL)
- ❏ Colors of Our World _____ _____
- ❏ Skit: How We Got Our Skin Color _____

1. _____
2. _____
3. _____
4. _____
5. _____
6. _____
7. _____

OVERCOMING PREJUDICE (30 min.)
- ❏ Song: God Is One (ALL)
- ❏ Felt lesson: Barriers into Bonds _____
- ❏ Song: I Am One Voice (All join in at 100 voices) _____
- ❏ Memory quote: "The earth is but one country…" _____
- ❏ Mini-opera: We Can Build a Beautiful World
- ❏ Crafts: Chocolate Rose _____ and Diversity Streamer _____
- ❏ Song: Glorious Day (ALL STAND)
- ❏ **Say**: We hope you liked our program. Please join us for refreshments!

The Power of Unity – Children's Performance

REHEARSAL GROUPS

Scripts and instructions are included on the following pages.

PROGRAM COORDINATOR: _____

- ❑ Select and orient 1 or 2 MCs. Provide a clipboard, pencil and copy of the agenda.
- ❑ Divide children into 3 groups and assign volunteers to each group (7-8 volunteers total).
- ❑ Make sure each child has at least one part in addition to the group songs.
- ❑ One or two children can be asked to play a short musical selection to begin the program.
- ❑ Songs can be practiced all together after group rehearsals and again after dinner.

Rehearse each part below with the children. The order will be different during the show.

GROUP #1: Demonstrations and Skit (very little speaking, easiest parts)
(2 youth or adults + 7 children)

- ❑ Stick and Bundle Demo *(see rehearsal notes)*
- ❑ Heavy Chair Demo *(see rehearsal notes)*
- ❑ Skit: "How We Got Our Skin Color"

1. _____
2. _____
3. _____
4. _____
5. _____
6. _____
7. _____

GROUP #2: Singing (mini-opera and other songs, medium difficulty)
(2-3 adults + 9 or more children)

- ❑ Musical Demo *(see rehearsal notes)*
- ❑ Song: "I Am One Voice" (select one child as the lead)
- ❑ Mini-opera: "We Can Build A Beautiful World"

GROUP #3: Speaking (variety of parts, medium difficulty and above)
If necessary, use children from the other groups after they have finished.
(3 youth or adults + 5 or more children)

- ❑ Short opening prayer _____
- ❑ Poem: "Hooray for Skin" _____
- ❑ Memory quotes (#1, 4, 7, 8, 14) _____ _____ _____ _____ _____
- ❑ Show each craft, explain how you made it and what it means (2-3 children each):

    Flowers of One Garden (poster) _____ _____ _____
    Leaf Laminate _____ _____ _____
    Chocolate Rose _____ _____ _____
    Diversity Streamer _____ _____ _____
    Personal Posters _____ _____ _____

- ❑ Short talk on "Unity in Diversity" (1 or 2 children) _____ _____
- ❑ Colors of Our World *(see rehearsal notes)* _____ _____
- ❑ Felt lesson: "The Eye" _____ _____
- ❑ Felt lesson: "Barriers into Bonds" _____ _____

1. _____
2. _____
3. _____
4. _____
5. _____
6. _____
7. _____
8. _____
9. _____

The Power of Unity – Children's Performance

REHEARSAL NOTES

Stick and Bundle Demo *(1 child)* _____

Materials: One thin stick, a lot of thin sticks tied together in a bundle

1. Ask an audience member to come up and try to break the stick. (It should be easy.)
2. Then give the same person the bundle of sticks to break. (This should be impossible.)
3. Ask: What can we learn from this? (There is strength in unity.)

Heavy Chair Pantomime *(5 children)* _____ _____ _____ _____ _____

Materials: A sturdy chair

1. Have one child sit silently in a sturdy chair at the front of the room.
2. Four other children enter and one by one, each tries to lift the chair without success. (They should struggle and grunt, hamming it up to show how difficult it is.)
3. Then the children consult, decide to work together to lift the chair with its occupant, carry it a few steps, gently set it down, congratulate each other, and take a bow.

Musical Demo *(1 child who can lead a song)* _____

1. Hum a single musical note and ask the audience to hum it with you. Then sing "Row, row, row your boat" (or other common song) with the audience, but tell them they can only use that one note. (The song will sound rather dull.) Explain that this is a demonstration of <u>**sameness**</u>. Bo-ring!

2. Next, tell the audience that when you give the signal, they should loudly make as many different noises as they can. You should hear screeching, squawking, cackling, hooting, hissing, howling, barking and other discordant sounds. Stop them after a few seconds, and explain that this is a demonstration of <u>**diversity without unity**</u>. It's what we have in the world today.

3. Then quickly divide the audience into three groups (approximately equal in size), and give each group one note of 3-note chord. The music leader can help with this. Have each group hum its note separately, then have all sing together for (hopefully) a pleasing sound. Explain that this is a demonstration of <u>**unity in diversity**</u>, and it takes practice.

"The diversity in the human family should be the cause of love and harmony, as it is in music where many different notes blend together in the making of a perfect chord." ('Abdu'l-Bahá, Paris Talks, p. 53)

Colors of Our World *(2 children)* _____ _____
Materials: Four color pictures (see Lesson #3, p. 59 and 70)

1. Explain to the audience that there are many types of pigments or colorings, that brighten our world:
   - **Carotene** pigment makes carrots and pumpkins orange.
   - **Chlorophyll** pigment makes leaves and grass green.
   - **Hemoglobin** pigment makes our blood red.
   - **Melanin** pigment makes our skin brown.

   While speaking, hold up a large color picture of each item. See examples below.

2. All people have melanin in their skin. Melanin protects us from the sun's harmful rays – as you will see in our next skit!

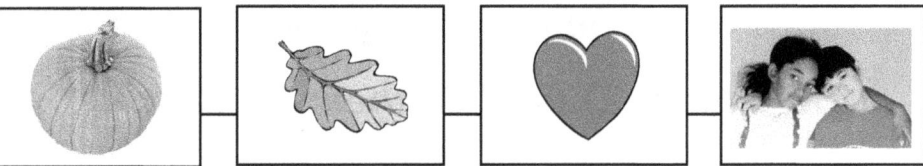

Short Talk on "Unity in Diversity" *(1 or 2 children)* _____ _____
Materials: The children can review their handouts on "Unity" (Lesson #1) and "Unity in Diversity" (Lesson #2) for ideas. Encourage them to speak naturally using their own words, rather than reading. They can make a sketch or write a few key words on a card as a memory aid.

Skit: "How We Got Our Skin Color" *(1 narrator + 6 easy parts = 7 children)*

_____ + _____ _____ _____ _____ _____ _____

1. Read through the skit with the group.
2. Ask for volunteers, audition the narrator, and assign parts.
3. Distribute costumes and props. (See script for list of materials.)
4. Rehearse the skit. (The narrator should practice with a microphone if needed.)

Opening Prayer

O my God! O my God!
Unite the hearts of Thy servants,
and reveal to them Thy great purpose.
May they follow Thy commandments
and abide in Thy law.
Help them, O God, in their endeavor,
and grant them strength to serve Thee.
O God! Leave them not to themselves,
but guide their steps
by the light of Thy knowledge,
and cheer their hearts by Thy love.
Verily, Thou art their Helper
and their Lord.

- Bahá'u'lláh

The Power of Unity – Children's Performance

Script for Felt Lesson

"The Eye"

	NARRATION	ACTION	
1	The eye is an example of unity in diversity.	Place large white eye in center of felt board.	
2	Each part of the eye has a different job, but they all work together for the same goal.	Place blue circle in center of eye; then add black circle on top.	
3	For example, the pupil is the black opening in front of the eye that admits light so we can see.	Point to black pupil.	
4	The iris opens and closes, changing the size of the pupil to let in just the right amount of light.	Point to blue iris.	
5	What would happen if all the parts of the eye were the same?	Place white circle over other circles.	

The parts of the eye are different, but they all work together, and all are necessary for sight.

The Power of Unity – Children's Performance

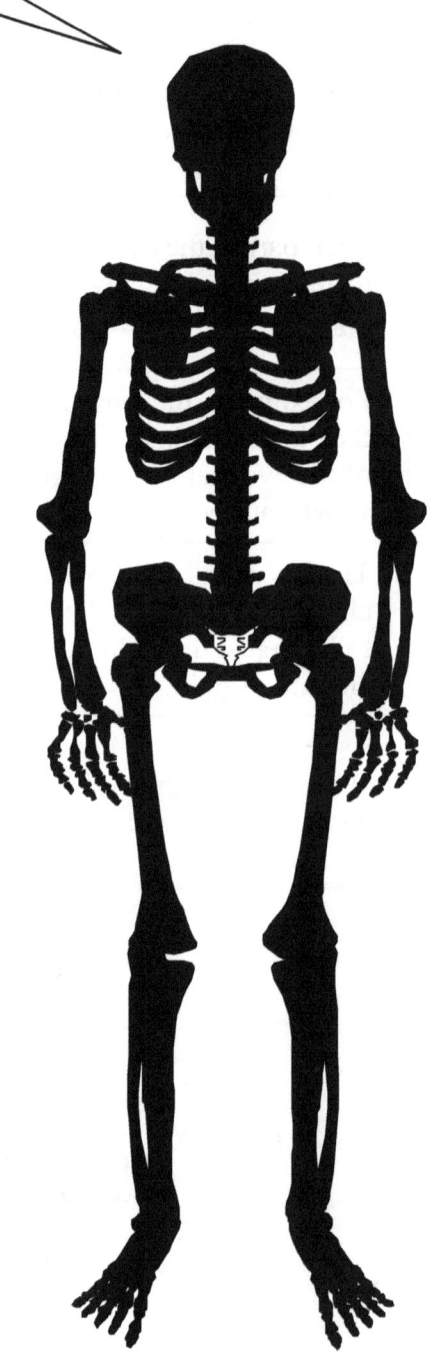

HOORAY FOR SKIN
by Susan Engle

Rejoice and celebrate the skin
That keeps the veins and muscles in,
That keeps the cold and germies out.
That is what skin is all about.

Suppose, when God created skin,
He turned the skinside outside-in.
So when you talk to Mrs. Jones,
Your eyes meet over fat and bones,
And tissues, blue and white and red,
That stretch from toe to hand to head.
It makes me glad to have a skin
To keep the outside boneside-in.

Now there are folks who would be mad
If our insides were all they had
To tell all kinds of folks apart.
Maybe they'd learn to read the heart
Instead of judging from a hue
If one man's false and one man's true.

Let's all join hands and feast our eyes
On skins of every shape and size,
Of every tone of gold or white,
Of luscious black, of dark or light,
Of every shade that folks come in.
Rejoice and celebrate the skin.

© 1986, Susan Engle. Used with permission.

The Power of Unity – Children's Performance

 # How We Got Our Skin Color

Materials

- ❏ Knee-high women's nylon stockings or socks (3 of medium shade, 1 dark, 1 light)
- ❏ Paper sun on pole (see next page)
- ❏ Strip of red cloth

Characters *(7 children)*

1. Narrator
2. Sun (child holding up sun on pole)
3. Sunburn Kid (with red cloth wrapped around one arm)
4. Weakbone Kid (walks slowly, bent over)
5. Three Melanin Kids (Each wears a medium shade nylon stocking on the right arm. In addition, the first child carries a dark nylon, and the third child wears a light nylon under the medium one.)

1. _____
2. _____
3. _____
4. _____
5. _____
6. _____
7. _____

Note: All characters enter from stage right (actor's right when facing audience) and exit stage left.

	NARRATION	ACTION
1	How did we get our skin color? We all need just the right amount of sunlight in order to survive.	Sun enters, moves to center stage.
2	Too much sun can cause sunburn, skin cancer or heatstroke.	Sunburn Kid enters with red arm hidden at first. Sun touches kid's arm, kid says "ouch!" and exits frowning.
3	Too little sun can cause weak bones.	Sun sets. Weakbone Kid limps across stage and exits frowning.
4	Melanin, the color in our skin, helps to block the sun's rays.	Sun rises. Melanin Kids enter together, line up in front of sun facing audience, with right arms out, smiling.
5	If your ancestors lived in a very warm climate, they developed more melanin in their skin to protect them from the hot sun.	Sun moves close to and "shines" on first kid, who adds a dark nylon over the medium nylon on right arm.
6	If your ancestors lived in a very cold climate, they developed less melanin in their skin so more sunlight could enter.	Third kid (farthest from the sun) removes medium nylon to reveal a light one underneath.
7	And that's how we got the colors of our skin.	Kids proudly show off their skin colors to the audience, then exit smiling.

Skit is based on concepts from the book, *All The Colors We Are* by Katie Kissinger.

The Power of Unity – Children's Performance

Sun pattern for skit on "How We Got Our Skin Color"

Cut from yellow paper.

1. Trace around this circle or a dinner plate, or draw a large circle on bright yellow paper, and cut out to make the sun.
2. Cut 8-10 yellow triangles to make the sun's rays.
3. Glue the sun and its rays onto the inside of a blue manila folder or blue poster board.
4. Using a permanent marker, draw a nose and a mouth on the sun.
5. Using a sharp point, poke two holes through the sun approximately where its eyes should be, and insert the temples (arms) of a real pair of sunglasses. (Use the glasses to measure for correct spacing of the holes.)
6. Add masking tape to the back of the poster to reinforce the holes.
7. Tape the poster to a yardstick, broom handle or other lightweight pole.
8. To store, remove the stick and glasses, and close the folder.

The Power of Unity – Children's Performance

Script for Felt Lesson

"Barriers into Bonds"

	NARRATION	ACTION
1	All around the world, people are different in many ways.	Place globe in center of felt board and add the people around it in a circle.
2	We have different skin colors, speak different languages, come from different cultures, live in different countries, and practice different religions.	As each difference is mentioned, place it above one of the people. 
3	Some people dislike others without even knowing them, just because of these differences. This is called prejudice. Because of prejudice, our differences have become barriers between us.	Place the barriers between the people. 
4	But Bahá'u'lláh says that the earth is one country and mankind its citizens.	Indicate the earth and all the people with a circular motion of your hand.
5	When we realize that we all belong to the same human family, we will see our differences as a source of beauty and strength, and these barriers will become bonds of unity.	Flip the barriers over and turn them sideways to form bonds. 
6	When the human family is united, the world will finally be at peace.	Add the dove above the earth.
7	Bahá'u'lláh says, "The well-being of mankind, its peace and security, are unattainable unless and until its unity is firmly established." *	

* Gleanings, p. 286

The Power of Unity – Children's Performance

We Can Build a Beautiful World

© Russ Garcia. Music excerpted and simplified.
Used with permission. See music section for sheet music.

Divide children into three groups with costumes as indicated below. Include choreographed gestures if desired. The audience can also be divided into three groups, given the words, and asked to join in.

Group A: Green people are the best. Far better than the rest.
We hate you because you're different!
We are superior, you are inferior.
We love us and we hate you, my friend.

Group B: Purple people are the best. Far better than the rest.
We hate you because you're different!
We are superior, you are inferior.
We love us and we hate you, my friend.

(Sung in a round)

A: Green people are the best. Far better than the rest.
B: (silent)

A: We hate you because you're different!
B: Purple people are the best. Far better than the rest.

A: We are superior, you are inferior.
B: We hate you because you're different!

A: We love us and we hate you, my…
B: We are superior, you are inferior.

A: …friend.
B: We love us and we hate you, my…
C: WE CAN BUILD A …

A: We love us and we hate you.
B: …friend.
C: BEAUTIFUL WORLD…

A: (silent)
B: We love us and we hate you.
C: WHEN WE LEARN THAT…

A: (silent)
B: (silent)
C: MANKIND IS ONE.

Costumes

Group A: Green T-shirts
Group B: Purple T-shirts
Group C: Red or multi-colored T-shirts

Sample Gestures

For Us: Thumbs up, pat heart, thumbs in lapels

For Them: Thumbs down, press palm out, hold nose

Unifiers: Help all join hands.

All: WE CAN HAVE A WONDERFUL WORLD, WHEN WE LEARN TO LOVE.

We can build a beautiful world,
When we learn the earth is one land.
We can have a wonderful world,
When we learn to love.

We can build a beautiful world,
When we learn to love all mankind.
We can have a wonderful world,
WHEN WE LEARN TO LOVE!
LOVE!! LOVE!!! LOVE!!!! LOVE!!!!!

Bahá'í Children's Classes and Retreats: Theme 5, p. 138

The Power of Unity – Children's Performance

Sample program for the audience

Bahá'í Children's Class Performance

The Power of Unity

"So powerful is the light of unity that it can illuminate the whole earth." —Bahá'u'lláh

Welcome

Opening music and prayers

The Power of Unity
- We are Drops (song)
- Stick and Bundle (demo)
- The Heavy Chair (skit)
- Memory quotes

Unity in Diversity
- Si Estamos Juntos (song)
- Memory quote
- Unity in Diversity (speech)
- Flowers of One Garden (craft)
- Leaf Laminates (craft)
- Musical demonstration
- The Eye (felt lesson)
- One Planet, One People (song)

The Colors We Are
- Hooray for Skin (poem)
- Personal posters
- Memory quote
- Good Neighbors Come in All Colors (song)
- Colors of Our World
- How We Got Our Skin Color (skit)

Overcoming Prejudice
- God Is One (song)
- Barriers into Bonds (felt lesson)
- I Am One Voice (song)
- Memory quote
- We Can Build a Beautiful World (mini-opera)
- Chocolate Rose (craft)
- Diversity Streamer (craft)
- Glorious Day (song)

Refreshments

Bahá'í Children's Classes and Retreats: Theme 5, p. 139

The Power of Unity – Children's Performance

A few photos from our children's class

Handouts

The student handouts from all of the lessons are included in this section for ease of photocopying. These handouts can also be downloaded from: www.UnityWorksStore.com > Children's Classes > The Power of Unity > student handouts.

The Power of Unity

HANDOUTS

Orientation and All Lessons

Song Sheet	143
Quotations	145
The Power of Unity (packet of readings)	147

LESSON #1: The Power of Unity

Unity Is / Disunity Is	149
Word Puzzles	150
Unity	151

LESSON #2: Unity in Diversity

Unity in Diversity	152
Unity in Diversity (instructions for group leaders)	46

LESSON #3: The Colors We Are

Class Features Chart	64
Hooray for Skin	153
Personal Poster (blank form)	69

LESSON #4: Overcoming Prejudice

The Sneetches	154
Personal Stories (instructions for group leaders)	82
Dealing with Putdowns and Prejudice	155
Name It, Claim It	156
The Black Rose	157
The Black Rose (instructions for group leaders)	85
Creating Unity	159

The Power of Unity

Name _____

SONG SHEET

Most of these songs are copyrighted and used with permission. See music section for details.

Hawaiian Unity Song
(Echo song; composer unknown)

We are drops of one ocean,
We are waves of one sea...

**Come and join us…
In our quest for unity,
It's a way of life for you and me.**

We are flowers of one garden.
We are leaves of one tree... (chorus)

Black and white, red and yellow,
Lovely colors of humanity... (chorus)

All the earth is one country,
We are one family... (chorus)

We are drops of one ocean,
We are waves of one sea... (chorus)

Si Estamos Juntos
(Spanish: The More We Sing Together)

Si estamos juntos,
Juntos, juntos.
Si estamos juntos,
Me siento feliz.

Tus amigos son míos,
Mis amigos son tuyos,
Si estamos juntos,
Me siento feliz.

Oh, Bahá'u'lláh
(by Greg Dahl)

Oh Bahá'u'lláh, (3x)
Bring us together in unity,
Bring us together as one family.

We are all waves of one sea,
We are all leaves of one tree,
We are all flowers of one garden,
Bring us together in unity,
Bring us together as one family.

God Is One
(by Margaret Jane King)

God is one, man is one,
And all the religions are one.
Land and sea, hill and valley,
Under the beautiful sun.

**God is one, man is one,
And all the religions agree.
When everyone learns
   the three onenesses,
We'll have world unity.**

God is love, God is light,
And all are as one in His sight.
Black and white, red and yellow,
Now is the time to unite. (chorus)

Dios Es Uno
(Spanish: God Is One)

Dios es uno, el hombre es uno,
Y las religiones también.
Tierra y mar, cerros y valles,
Bajo el hermoso sol.

Dios es uno, el hombre es uno,
Y las religiones concuerdan.
Cuando todos aprenden las tres verdades,
Habrá unidad mundial.

I Am One Voice
(by Don Eaton)

I am one voice, I am singing (3x)
I am not alone.

- We are two voices, we are singing…
- We are three voices…
- We are ten voices…
- We are twenty voices…
- We are a hundred voices…
- We are one voice…

The Power of Unity

What Mankind Has to Learn
(by Creadell Haley)

There's only One God,
throughout the universe,
But man multiplied Him and so…
There's a your God and my God,
What mankind has to learn,
Is that there's only One God to know.

There's only One Race
of people on the earth,
But man did divide it and so…
There's a Black race, a White race,
What mankind has to learn,
Is that there's only One Race to know.

Earth was One Country
when God gave it to man,
But man did divide it and so…
There's a China, a Turkey,
What mankind has to learn,
Is that Earth is One Country to know.

There's only Oneness
throughout the world of God,
But man won't believe it and so…
He divides and multiplies it,
Oh won't he ever learn,
That there's only Oneness to know.

One Planet, One People
(Echo song by Sandee English)

One planet, one people,
We all live together.
One planet, one people, please.

All the world is full of people,
And our hearts all beat as one.
Though we're different from each other,
We're illumined by the rays of just one sun.
      (chorus)

We are flowers of one garden,
We are leaves of just one tree.
Though we're different from each other,
We're illumined by the light of unity.
      (chorus)

Good Neighbors
(by Dick Grover)

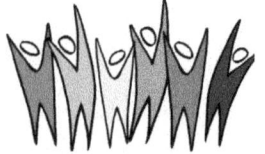

Good neighbors come in all colors,
Black, red, yellow and tan.
Our outsides may look different,
But we're the family of Woman and Man.

When my doorbell starts to ring,
I can't see the ringer's skin.
Even if he had bright blue skin,
I'd welcome him right in. (chorus)

When my neighbor starts to cry,
That hurts him and that hurts I.
Even if he had orange eyes,
It hurts him when he cries. (chorus)

When my neighbor starts to share,
Joy and happiness everywhere,
Even if she had purple hair,
I wouldn't even care. (chorus)

Glorious Day
(by Steve and Shelley Hines)

All these faces, so much love.
Isn't this what we've been dreamin' of.
All are welcome, come on in.
Join hands, let the new day begin, singin'…

Oh, what a glorious, glorious, glorious,
Oh, what a wonderful glorious day, yeah!
God is most glorious, glorious, glorious,
Oh, what a wonderful glorious day!

Look to the future. It shall be done.
We're finally learnin' that mankind is one.
All together, side by side.
Everybody diversified, singin'… (chorus)

Hand in hand, heart to heart.
Build a bond that will never part. (chorus)

The Power of Unity

Quotations from the Bahá'í Writings on

UNITY & ONENESS

Class #1

(1) So powerful is the light of unity that it can illuminate the whole earth.
(Bahá'u'lláh, G, p. 288)

(2) O my God! O my God! Unite the hearts of Thy servants…
(Bahá'u'lláh, Bahá'í Prayers, p. 203)

(3) For thousands of years we have had bloodshed and strife. It is enough…Now is the time to associate together in love and harmony. *('Abdu'l-Bahá, PUP, p. 31)*

(4) The well-being of mankind, its peace and security, are unattainable unless and until its unity is firmly established. *(Bahá'u'lláh, G, p. 286)*

(5) O CHILDREN OF MEN! Know ye not why We created you all from the same dust? *(Bahá'u'lláh, HW #68)*

(6) All humanity are the children of God; they belong to the same family, to the same original race. *('Abdu'l-Bahá, PUP, p. 298)*

(7) The earth is but one country, and mankind its citizens. *(Bahá'u'lláh, G, p. 250)*

Class #2

(8) …regard ye not one another as strangers. Ye are the fruits of one tree, and the leaves of one branch… *('Abdu'l-Bahá, DAL, p. 114)*

(9) O Lord God! Make us as waves of the sea, as flowers of the garden, united, agreed through the bounties of Thy love. *('Abdu'l-Bahá, PUP, p.235)*

(10) Behold a beautiful garden full of flowers… Each flower has a different charm, a peculiar beauty, its own delicious perfume and beautiful colour… It is just the diversity and variety that constitutes its charm… *('Abdu'l-Bahá, PT, p. 52-3)*

(11) Thus should it be among the children of men! The diversity in the human family should be the cause of love and harmony, as it is in music where many different notes blend together in the making of a perfect chord. *('Abdu'l-Bahá, PT, p. 53)*

(12) If you meet those of a different race and colour from yourself…think of them as different coloured roses growing in the beautiful garden of humanity, and rejoice to be among them. *('Abdu'l-Bahá, PT, p. 53)*

The Power of Unity

Class #3

(13) Adam was of one color. Eve had one color. All humanity is descended from them. Therefore, in origin they are one. These colors developed later due to climates and regions; they have no significance whatsoever. *('Abdu'l-Bahá, PUP, p. 45)*

(14) God does not look at colors; He looks at the hearts. *('Abdu'l-Bahá, PUP, p. 44)*

Class #4

(15) All prejudices, whether of religion, race, politics or nation, must be renounced, for these prejudices have caused the world's sickness. *('Abdu'l-Bahá, PT, p. 146)*

(16) Throughout the animal kingdom we do not find the creatures separated because of color. They recognize unity of species and oneness of kind. If we do not find color distinction drawn in a kingdom of lower intelligence and reason, how can it be justified among human beings... *('Abdu'l-Bahá, FWU, p. 34)*

(17) For God created us all of one race....In the sight of God there is no difference between the various races. Why should man invent such a prejudice? *('Abdu'l-Bahá, PT, p.148)*

(18) Close your eyes to racial differences, and welcome all with the light of oneness. *(Bahá'u'lláh, quoted in Shoghi Effendi, ADJ, p. 37)*

(19) Be in perfect unity. Never become angry with one another. Love the creatures for the sake of God… *('Abdu'l-Bahá, PUP, p. 92)*

(20) …be a friend to the whole human race. *('Abdu'l-Bahá, SAB, p. 169)*

(21) Fellowship is the cause of unity, and unity is the source of order in the world. *(Bahá'u'lláh, Bahá'í Scriptures, p. 157)*

(22) We work and pray for the unity of mankind, that all the races of the earth may become one race, all the countries one country, and that all hearts may beat as one heart. *('Abdu'l-Bahá, PT, p. 100)*

References

ADJ	The Advent of Divine Justice
DAL	Divine Art of Living
FWU	Foundations of World Unity
G	Gleanings from the Writings of Bahá'u'lláh
HW	Hidden Words
PT	Paris Talks
PUP	The Promulgation of Universal Peace
SAB	Selections from the Writings of 'Abdu'l-Bahá

THE POWER OF UNITY

Name: _____

The Power of Unity – Handouts

These student handouts, along with full-page color illustrations designed to accompany the lessons, are available for download from: **www.UnityWorksStore.com**. Click on Children's Classes > The Power of Unity > student handouts. Illustrations can be posted on the wall during classes as an aid for visual learners and to help bring the lessons and readings to life.

Unity Is:

- Knowing that humankind is one family
- Treating all people with respect
- Valuing diversity
- Serving others
- Consulting together
- Making sure everyone is included
- Listening and trying to understand
- Working to make things better for all
- Solving conflicts peacefully
- Loving others, even when they aren't perfect
- Showing cooperation and teamwork
- Forgiving people
- Making friends

Disunity Is:

- Being selfish
- Insisting on your own way
- Not getting along with others
- Thinking you are better than everyone else
- Showing prejudice and hatred
- Shouting at people
- Telling lies about others
- Leaving people out
- Name calling and putdowns
- Laughing when someone makes a mistake
- Arguing or fighting
- Hurting other people
- Not caring about others
- Backbiting

The Power of Unity – Handouts

WORD PUZZLES

How many can you solve on your own?

1	2	3	4
SAND	MAN / BOARD	STAND / I	DICE DICE
5	6	7	8
WEAR / LONG	R O ROADS D S	RIGHT TIME	CYCLE CYCLE CYCLE

Bahá'í Children's Classes and Retreats: Theme 5, p. 150

UNITY

"The earth is but one country, and mankind its citizens."
(Bahá'u'lláh, Gleanings, p. 250)

One Human Family: There is only one race of people in the world. Do you know what it is called? That's right! It's the human race, and we all belong to it. We come in different shapes, sizes and colors, but we are one human family, children of one God.

We may be young or old, short or tall, male or female. We may have dark skin, light skin, or a color in-between. Some of us were born in China, South Africa, India or Brazil. We may speak English, Spanish, Arabic or Japanese. Some of us are good at sports, others at math, music or art. Some are Christians, Jews, Hindus, Muslims or Bahá'ís. We are diverse in many ways, but we live on one planet. One God created us all.

The Importance of Unity: Bahá'u'lláh tells us that God wants His children to live in unity. We should treat each other with justice and love. He said the whole human race was created from the same dust, so no one should look down on anyone else. Bahá'u'lláh says that countries must stop fighting wars and all people must work together for peace. But we won't have peace, until we first have unity. We must be united with our brothers and sisters all around the world.

"The well-being of mankind, its peace and security, are unattainable unless and until its unity is firmly established."
(Bahá'u'lláh, Gleanings, p. 286)

We Are Connected: People who understand unity know that everything in the whole universe is connected. Everything depends on something else to live. Animals must eat other animals or plants in order to survive. Plants need sunshine and rain to grow. Human beings are also connected to each other like links in a chain. Everything we do affects our planet and the other people on it. Every link is important. You are one of the links in that chain.

The Power of Unity: Unity is a powerful force that can connect us all. It can connect our families, communities and nations. Unity gives us strength. We are more powerful working together than alone. Unity is like medicine for the world's sickness. Unity will bring peace, progress and light to the world.

"So powerful is the light of unity that it can illuminate the whole earth."
(Bahá'u'lláh, Gleanings, p. 288)

UNITY IN DIVERSITY

"Be as one spirit, one soul, leaves of one tree, flowers of one garden..."
('Abdu'l-Bahá, Promulgation of Universal Peace, p. 24)

Imagine the flowers in a garden. 'Abdu'l-Bahá says that each flower has a different shape, its own special color and sweet-smelling perfume. But they all grow from the same earth, the same sun shines upon them, and the same clouds give them rain. Each flower is pleasing by itself, but when the different flowers are all together, the garden is even more beautiful.

It is the same with people. We are like beautiful flowers growing in a garden. We each have a different shape and our own special color. We speak different languages, wear different clothing, and enjoy different music and food. But we all live upon the same earth, breathe the same air, and are children of the same heavenly Father. Our diversity adds beauty to garden of humanity.

The Value of Diversity

- Think of all the colors in nature. Can you name some of them?
- Can you imagine if the entire world were all <u>one</u> color? Which color should it be?
- Would a rainbow be as beautiful if all the bands were the same shade?
- Could you bake a cake with only one ingredient?
- What if all the musical instruments in an orchestra made the same sound?

Just think how dull it would be if all people everywhere looked and acted and thought and talked and dressed exactly the same! What if you had to eat the same food every day, wear the same clothes, read the same books and think the same thoughts, for the rest of your life? What if you never, <u>ever</u> got to try anything new? And what if all your friends were exactly like you?

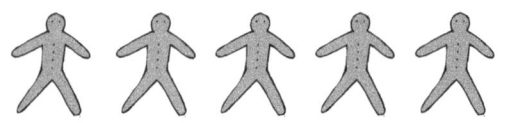

Diversity is important because it gives us beauty, variety, choices and new ideas.

Unity Is Not Sameness

Unity does not mean sameness. Unity means respecting our differences and working together in harmony. It means knowing that each part has something valuable to contribute to the whole. Each member of the human family has something special to offer to the human race.

When we have **unity in diversity**, there is harmony, like the sound of different notes joined together in a perfect chord. We are showing unity in diversity, when we all work and play and live together in peace.

HOORAY FOR SKIN
by Susan Engle

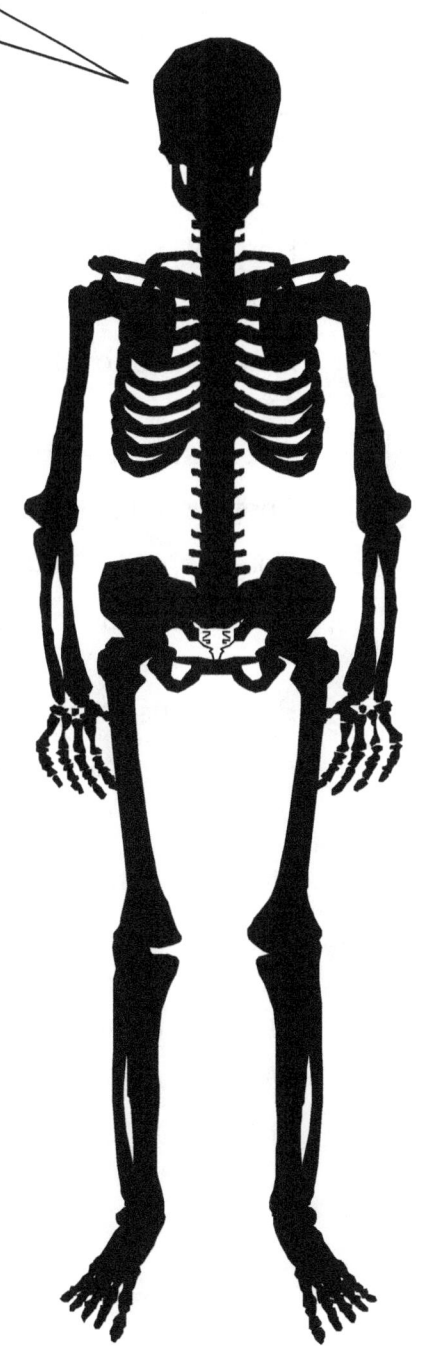

Rejoice and celebrate the skin
That keeps the veins and muscles in,
That keeps the cold and germies out.
That is what skin is all about.

Suppose, when God created skin,
He turned the skinside outside-in.
So when you talk to Mrs. Jones,
Your eyes meet over fat and bones,
And tissues, blue and white and red,
That stretch from toe to hand to head.
It makes me glad to have a skin
To keep the outside boneside-in.

Now there are folks who would be mad
If our insides were all they had
To tell all kinds of folks apart.
Maybe they'd learn to read the heart
Instead of judging from a hue
If one man's false and one man's true.

Let's all join hands and feast our eyes
On skins of every shape and size,
Of every tone of gold or white,
Of luscious black, of dark or light,
Of every shade that folks come in.
Rejoice and celebrate the skin.

© 1986, Susan Engle. Used with permission.

The Sneetches

From *The Sneetches and Other Stories* by Dr. Seuss.

TM & copyright © by Dr. Seuss Enterprises, L.P, 1953, 1954, 1961, renewed 1989.
Used by permission of Random House Children's Books, a division of Random House, Inc.

Now the Star-Belly Sneetches
Had bellies with stars.
The Plain-Belly Sneetches
Had none upon thars.

Those stars weren't so big
They were really so small.
You might think such a thing
Wouldn't matter at all.

But because they had stars
All the Star-Belly Sneetches
Would brag, "We're the best kind
Of Sneetches on beaches."

With their snoots in the air,
They would sniff and they'd snort
"We'll have nothing to do with
The Plain-Belly sort!"

And whenever they met some
When they were out walking,
They'd hike right on past them
Without even talking….

When the Star-Belly Sneetches
Had frankfurter roasts
Or picnics or parties
Or marshmallow toasts,

They never invited
The Plain-Belly Sneetches.
They left them out cold
In the dark on the beaches.

They kept them away.
Never let them come near.
And that's how they treated them
Year after year…

Dealing With
PUTDOWNS AND PREJUDICE

If someone calls you a name:
- Stay calm.
- Say, "I don't like it when you say that."
- Say, "That's mean. Please don't do it again!"
- Walk away.
- Tell some friends.
- Tell an adult.

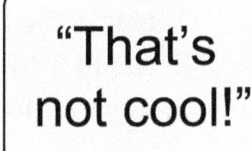
"That's not cool!"

Things to say to someone else who is called a name:
- It was wrong of her to say that about you. Are you okay?
- Can I help you report it to the teacher?
- Would you like to eat lunch with us from now on?

Ways to respond to prejudiced remarks:
- In our house, those words are not allowed.
- You're too nice a person to hurt someone like that.
- That's not okay. It's disrespectful to Native Americans.
- I don't like it when you say that. It's mean to girls.
- What makes you believe that about Arabs?
- Do you really mean what you said? Here's what I understood…
- I don't like that kind of joke. It puts down my family – the human family.

Try some *put-ups*:
- Nice to see you!
- Come and join us.
- You can do it.
- Good job!
- You look nice today.
- I like the way you shared your game.
- You were very helpful just now.
- Would you like to be friends?

The Power of Unity – Handouts

NAME IT, CLAIM IT, STOP IT

Adapted from a workshop given by Peggy Federici, Camp Peace, Idaho

"Name It, Claim It, Stop It" is another strategy for dealing with putdowns and prejudice. When you hear a biased remark, you can respond with three simple statements:

1. Name the biased behavior.
2. Claim it by stating how it makes <u>you</u> feel.
3. Tell the person to stop.

Here's an example:

Biased remark: "How many green people does it take to change a light bulb?"
Name It: "That's a racist joke."
Claim It: "I don't like it when you put down green people like that."
Stop It: "Please don't tell those jokes at our school."

See if you can label all three parts in the example below:

Biased remark: "I don't like purple people. They're all stupid!"

1. "What you just said about purple people – that's prejudice." _____
2. "It makes me sad to hear you say things like that." _____
3. "Please don't talk that way around me." _____

Now try your own example:

Biased remark: "_____"

Name It: _____
Claim It: _____
Stop It: _____

Practice with your partner and be ready to act out your example for the class.

The Black Rose

One day, when 'Abdu'l-Bahá was visiting a very poor section of New York, a large group of boys gathered around Him. Some threw sticks and called Him names. Mrs. Kinney, one of the local Bahá'ís who was with 'Abdu'l-Bahá, dropped behind to speak with the boys. She explained that He was a very Holy Man who had spent many years in prison because of His love for truth and for all people. She invited the boys to her house to personally meet 'Abdu'l-Bahá.

When they arrived, 'Abdu'l-Bahá was standing at the door. He welcomed each one, sometimes with a handshake, sometimes with an arm around a shoulder, but always with such smiles and laughter that it almost seemed He was a boy with them. The young visitors felt right at home.

One of the last to enter the room was a boy of African descent, about 13 years old. Because he was the only one in the group with very dark skin, he thought he might not be welcome. But when 'Abdu'l-Bahá saw the boy, His face lit up with a heavenly smile. He raised His hand in greeting and exclaimed in a loud voice so everyone could hear, that here was a black rose.

Suddenly, everyone was silent. The black child's face was shining with happiness and love. He had probably been called many things in his short life, but never a black rose. The other boys looked at him with new eyes.

'Abdu'l-Bahá had a large box of expensive chocolates brought in for the boys. He carried it around the room Himself, giving each boy a large handful of candy, with a word and a smile for everyone. Then He set the box down and picked out a very dark piece of chocolate.

He looked at it for a moment and then at the boys who were watching Him intently. Without a word 'Abdu'l-Bahá walked across the room to where the black boy was sitting, and with a piercing glance that swept the group, laid the dark chocolate against the black cheek.

'Abdu'l-Bahá's face was radiant as He laid His arm around the shoulder of the boy. That radiance seemed to fill the room. No words were necessary to convey His meaning, and there was no doubt that all of the boys understood.

 Not only was the boy a black flower, but also a black sweet. You eat chocolates and find them good: perhaps you would also find this black brother of yours good – once you taste his sweetness.

Again the room fell silent, and the boy himself gazed at 'Abdu'l-Bahá with such love in his eyes that he seemed transformed. The reality of his being had been brought to the surface and the angel he really was, revealed.

To the few Bahá'ís in the room, the scene brought visions of a new world in which every soul would be treated as a child of God.

(Adapted from Howard Colby Ives, *Portals to Freedom*, p. 65-67)

Study Questions

1. What was 'Abdu'l-Bahá doing when he met the group of boys?
2. Why do you think the boys threw sticks and called 'Abdu'l-Bahá names?
3. Who was Mrs. Kinney and why did she invite the boys to her home?
4. How did 'Abdu'l-Bahá greet the boys when they arrived?
5. Why did one boy think he might not be welcome?
6. What did 'Abdu'l-Bahá do when that boy entered the room?
7. How did people react to 'Abdu'l-Bahá's announcement, and why?
8. What did 'Abdu'l-Bahá do with the chocolate candy?
9. Without using any words, what did 'Abdu'l-Bahá teach the people in the room?
10. How did 'Abdu'l-Bahá's message affect the young boy?
11. What can we learn from the example of 'Abdu'l-Bahá?

CREATING UNITY

 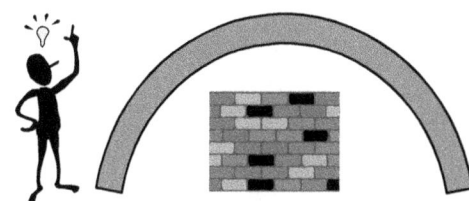

> Your group will be assigned one or more of the situations below. For each one, read and discuss it with your group. Then act it out twice—first the wrong way, then in a more positive way that creates unity. You can refer to the handouts on "Putdowns and Prejudice" and "Name It, Claim It, Stop It" for ideas. Be ready to perform your role plays for the class.

1. There is a new student at school. She always eats lunch by herself and doesn't seem to have any friends. Today, you see her sitting alone again.

2. On the bus to school, some older kids are teasing a boy who is overweight. They call him "fatso" and say they are going to beat him up after school.

3. All the kids are going to the fair after school. Two of your friends don't have enough money to go.

4. While walking home from school, you pass a group of younger students who are laughing and telling jokes about people who speak with accents.

5. You and your friends sit together every day at lunch. There is an open space at your table and a new girl sits down to eat. After she leaves, the others make fun of her hair and clothing.

6. You are helping out with chores around the house when your brother's friend bumps into you and calls you a stupid idiot.

7. There is a student from Japan in your class. Before class begins, some of the other students tease him, laughing at the shape of his eyes.

8. During recess, the boys decide to play hide-and-seek. A girl wants to join them, but they say that girls aren't allowed to play.

9. After dinner, your brothers and sisters all want to watch different television shows at the same time.

10. Your teacher passes out feathers for an art project. Several classmates stick the feathers in their hair and dance around wildly, making war whoops and shouting, "Me, Indian!"

11. At Bahá'í school, a little girl tries to say a prayer, but the words are very hard for her and some of the other children laugh at her mistakes.

12. An older boy and his younger brother are at a Holy Day observance. The child is bored and wiggles around making noise. Big brother hits him and loudly tells him to shut up. The child starts crying.

Music

"The art of music is divine and effective. It is the food of the soul and spirit.
Through the power and charm of music the spirit of man is uplifted.
It has wonderful sway and effect in the hearts of children,
for their hearts are pure, and melodies have great influence in them."

'Abdu'l-Bahá, The Promulgation of Universal Peace, p. 52

The Power of Unity – Music

Music Program

*"We, verily, have made music as a ladder for your souls,
a means whereby they may be lifted up unto the realm on high…"*

(Baha'u'llah, Kitáb-i-Aqdas, p. 38)

To the Music Coordinator

Singing brings people together for an enjoyable activity. It uplifts the souls and connects the hearts. It is also an excellent tool for memorizing information and for teaching and reinforcing new ideas.

The songs included in this teacher's guide have been selected to help children learn about unity. The students should have song sheets in their folders. As the music coordinator, your job is to help them learn some of these songs.

If the children's classes are held during a weekend retreat format, a morning sing-a-long has been scheduled each day for this purpose. There are also opportunities for singing after lunch and in the evenings. Classroom teachers may ask for your assistance with music that is part of their class. In addition, the music coordinator should help with the children's performance and the rehearsal. Check with the organizers for a schedule with the exact times.

As the song leader, you should be enthusiastic, confident and encouraging. Be patient with children who are shy or who don't catch on right away. When teaching a song for the first time, you will need to sing slowly, with a lot of repetition. If you play an instrument, you can bring it with you to accompany the singing and to keep the beat.

Be sure to learn the songs and the correct meaning and pronunciation of all the words beforehand, and arrive early so your session starts on time. Bring a music stand if available.

A song sheet and musical scores are included on the following pages. Some of the selections have been simplified and shortened for group singing with children. If you know a different melody for a particular song, use the version you feel most comfortable with. Songs in other languages have been included and may be used if desired.

To start a sing-a-long session:

- Ask the children to take out their song sheets and find the first song.
- Ask them what they think the song is about, and explain if necessary.
- Pronounce and define any difficult words.
- Play the song through once, encouraging those who know it to sing with you.
- If necessary, have children repeat each line in a speaking voice before trying to sing.
- Give the starting note and play or clap out the rhythm while everyone sings.
- Practice several times before going on to the next song.

The Power of Unity – Music

Transposing a Song

> Idea from Dick Grover

If the notes of a song are too high or too low to sing comfortably, you can easily change the song to a new key – called *transposing*. On a guitar, the easiest way to change the key is by using a capo. You can also follow the steps below.

1. Start by determining the original key (usually the first chord on the sheet music). Play that chord and sing a few lines of the song. If it is too high or too low, you will need to find a more comfortable key.

2. Play a different chord and try singing the song in that key. If it feels comfortable, you have found the right key. If not, play another chord and sing a few lines until you have found a comfortable key to sing in. You will transpose the song to that key. For example, if the song is too low in the original key of D but feels just right in the key of G, you will transpose the entire song to the key of G.

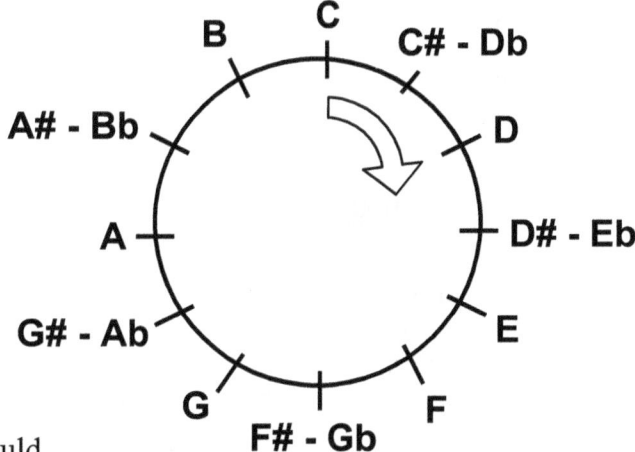

3. Using the chart and moving clockwise, count the number of steps from the original chord to the transposed chord. For example, there are five steps from D to G.

4. Then go through the entire song, changing all the chords by the same number of steps. Based on our example, you would raise all the D chords to G. All the E chords would change to A. An A7 would become a D7, etc. Write the new chord directly over the syllable you will be singing with that chord, or you will be out of rhythm when you play the song.

means "sharp" (It raises that note by a half step.)

b means "flat" (It lowers that note by a half step.)

C# and Db are the same note and count together as one step.
This is also true for D# and Eb, F# and Gb, G# and Ab, A# and Bb.

Bahá'í Children's Classes and Retreats: Theme 5, p. 163

The Power of Unity – Music   Name _____

SONG SHEET

Most of these songs are copyrighted and used with permission. See music section for details.

Hawaiian Unity Song
(Echo song; composer unknown)

We are drops of one ocean,
We are waves of one sea...

**Come and join us...
In our quest for unity,
It's a way of life for you and me.**

We are flowers of one garden.
We are leaves of one tree... (chorus)

Black and white, red and yellow,
Lovely colors of humanity... (chorus)

All the earth is one country,
We are one family... (chorus)

We are drops of one ocean,
We are waves of one sea... (chorus)

Si Estamos Juntos
(Spanish: The More We Sing Together)

Si estamos juntos,
Juntos, juntos.
Si estamos juntos,
Me siento feliz.

Tus amigos son míos,
Mis amigos son tuyos,
Si estamos juntos,
Me siento feliz.

Oh, Bahá'u'lláh
(by Greg Dahl)

Oh Bahá'u'lláh, (3x)
Bring us together in unity,
Bring us together as one family.

We are all waves of one sea,
We are all leaves of one tree,
We are all flowers of one garden,
Bring us together in unity,
Bring us together as one family.

God Is One
(by Margaret Jane King)

God is one, man is one,
And all the religions are one.
Land and sea, hill and valley,
Under the beautiful sun.

**God is one, man is one,
And all the religions agree.
When everyone learns
   the three onenesses,
We'll have world unity.**

God is love, God is light,
And all are as one in His sight.
Black and white, red and yellow,
Now is the time to unite. (chorus)

Dios Es Uno
(Spanish: God Is One)

Dios es uno, el hombre es uno,
Y las religiones también.
Tierra y mar, cerros y valles,
Bajo el hermoso sol.

Dios es uno, el hombre es uno,
Y las religiones concuerdan.
Cuando todos aprenden las tres verdades,
Habrá unidad mundial.

I Am One Voice
(by Don Eaton)

I am one voice, I am singing (3x)
I am not alone.

- We are two voices, we are singing...
- We are three voices...
- We are ten voices...
- We are twenty voices...
- We are a hundred voices...
- We are one voice...

Bahá'í Children's Classes and Retreats: Theme 5, p. 164

What Mankind Has to Learn
(by Creadell Haley)

There's only One God,
throughout the universe,
But man multiplied Him and so…
There's a your God and my God,
What mankind has to learn,
Is that there's only One God to know.

There's only One Race
of people on the earth,
But man did divide it and so…
There's a Black race, a White race,
What mankind has to learn,
Is that there's only One Race to know.

Earth was One Country
when God gave it to man,
But man did divide it and so…
There's a China, a Turkey,
What mankind has to learn,
Is that Earth is One Country to know.

There's only Oneness
throughout the world of God,
But man won't believe it and so…
He divides and multiplies it,
Oh won't he ever learn,
That there's only Oneness to know.

One Planet, One People
(Echo song by Sandee English)

**One planet, one people,
We all live together.
One planet, one people, please.**

All the world is full of people,
And our hearts all beat as one.
Though we're different from each other,
We're illumined by the rays of just one sun.
      (chorus)

We are flowers of one garden,
We are leaves of just one tree.
Though we're different from each other,
We're illumined by the light of unity.
      (chorus)

Good Neighbors
(by Dick Grover)

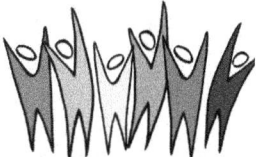

**Good neighbors come in all colors,
Black, red, yellow and tan.
Our outsides may look different,
But we're the family of Woman and Man.**

When my doorbell starts to ring,
I can't see the ringer's skin.
Even if he had bright blue skin,
I'd welcome him right in. (chorus)

When my neighbor starts to cry,
That hurts him and that hurts I.
Even if he had orange eyes,
It hurts him when he cries. (chorus)

When my neighbor starts to share,
Joy and happiness everywhere,
Even if she had purple hair,
I wouldn't even care. (chorus)

Glorious Day
(by Steve and Shelley Hines)

All these faces, so much love.
Isn't this what we've been dreamin' of.
All are welcome, come on in.
Join hands, let the new day begin, singin'…

**Oh, what a glorious, glorious, glorious,
Oh, what a wonderful glorious day, yeah!
God is most glorious, glorious, glorious,
Oh, what a wonderful glorious day!**

Look to the future. It shall be done.
We're finally learnin' that mankind is one.
All together, side by side.
Everybody diversified, singin'… (chorus)

Hand in hand, heart to heart.
Build a bond that will never part. (chorus)

The Power of Unity – Music

SONGS ABOUT UNITY

1. Glorious Day ………………………………..	167
2. God Is One ………………………………….	168
3. Dios Es Uno ………………………………...	169
4. Good Neighbors ……………………………	170
5. Hawaiian Unity Song ……………………..	171
6. I Am One Voice ……………………………	172
7. Oh, Bahá'u'lláh (Bring Us Together in Unity) ……	173
8. One Planet, One People …………………..	174
9. Si Estamos Juntos …………………………	175
10. What Mankind Has to Learn ……………..	176
11. We Can Build a Beautiful World* ………..	177

The children may also enjoy singing along with several wonderful Red Grammer songs about unity. The lyrics for *Teaching Peace, Rapp Song, Listen, I Think You're Wonderful, With Two Wings, Places in the World* and other songs can be found at: **www.redgrammer. com**. Click on Store and Lyrics. These songs are from "Teaching Peace," Red's award-winning children's recording. The songs can also be purchased separately from: **www.apple.com/itunes.**

Acknowledgements

Our deepest gratitude goes to Jonathan Gottlieb for transcribing the music for these songs. Appreciation to Tony Lee for permission to use the Hawaiian Unity Song that first appeared in: *Building Bridges: A Bahá'í Songbook,* by Peggy Caton and Dale Nomura, for the U.S. Bahá'í National Education Committee, published by Kalimát Press: Los Angeles, 1984.

"Glorious Day," a children's favorite by Steve and Shelley Hines, is available from: www.divinenotes.com. Enter "glorious day" in the search box.

Don Eaton's beautiful song, "One Voice," is available on CD. For information on Don's CDs and concert bookings, contact him at: eatonsong@aol.com or: www.small-change.org.

Dick Grover, composer of "Good Neighbors Come in All Colors," has a CD full of delightful children's songs which can be ordered while supplies last at: dijagro@teleport.com.

Two songs, "Si Estamos Juntos" and "Dios Es Uno" are Spanish translations from the English. The translators are unknown.

Some of the songs have been simplified and shortened for the purpose of group singing with children. A few of the songs have passed into the realm of Bahá'í folk music and their origins have been lost. We would be pleased to hear from any composers we have been unable to locate.

* For the children's performance

God Is One

Margaret Jane King

Baha'i Children's Classes and Retreats: Theme 5, p. 168

Dios Es Uno

**From "God Is One"
by Margaret Jane King
Spanish; translator unknown**

Baha'i Children's Classes and Retreats: Theme 5, p. 169

Hawaiian Unity Song
(Echo Song)

Composer Unknown
From Building Bridges songbook
Used with permission

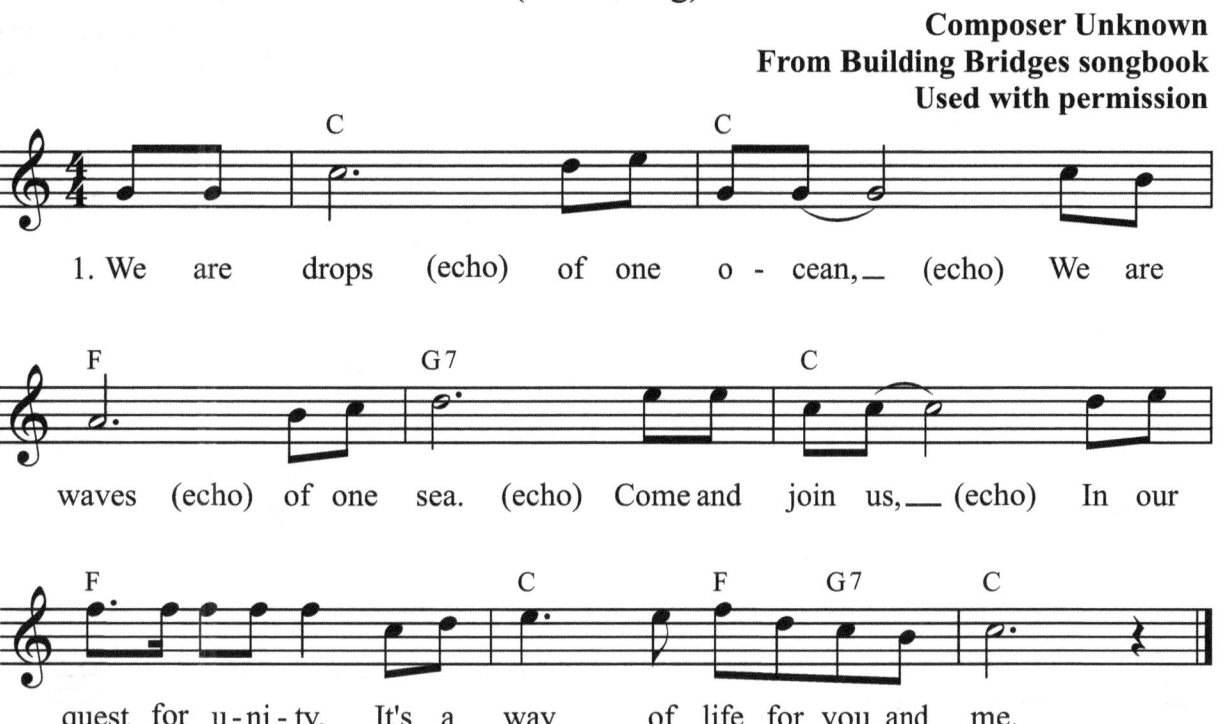

1. We are drops (echo) of one ocean, (echo) We are waves (echo) of one sea. (echo) Come and join us, (echo) In our quest for u-ni-ty, It's a way of life for you and me.

CHORUS (together):
In our quest for unity.
It's a way of life for you and me.

2. We are flowers, of one garden.
   We are leaves, of one tree... (chorus)

3. Black and white, red and yellow,
   Lovely colors, of humanity... (chorus)

4. All the earth, is one country,
   We are one, family... (chorus)

5. We are drops, of one ocean,
   We are waves, of one sea... (chorus)

I Am One Voice

(c) 2002 Don Eaton
All rights reserved
Used with permission

I am one voice,___ I am sing-ing.___ I am one voice,

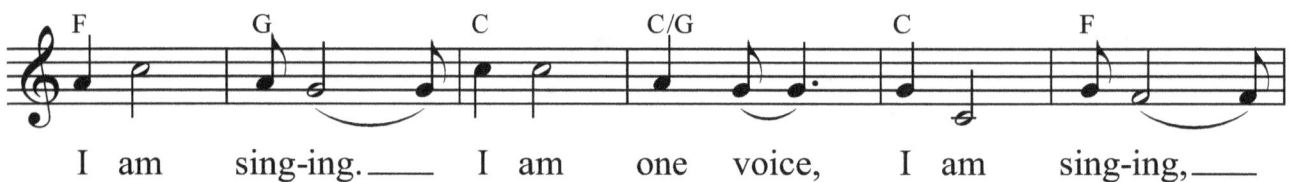

I am sing-ing.___ I am one voice, I am sing-ing,___

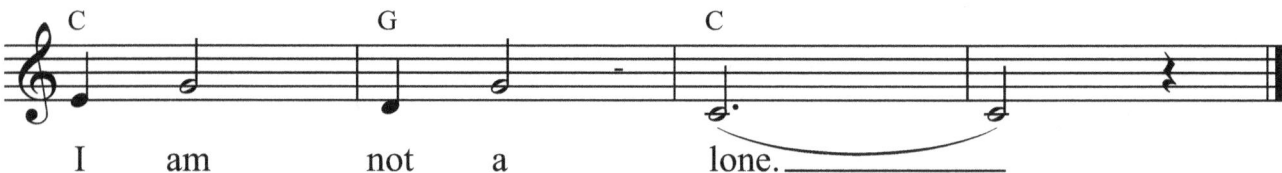

I am not a lone.___

2. We are two voices, we are singing. (3 times) We are not alone.

3. We are three voices, we are singing. (3 times) We are not alone.

4. We are four voices, we are singing. (3 times) We are not alone.

5. We are five voices, we are singing. (3 times) We are not alone.

6. We are ten voices, we are singing. (3 times) We are not alone.

7. We are twenty-five voices, we are singing. (3 times) We are not alone.

8. We are fifty voices, we are singing. (3 times) We are not alone.

9. We are one hundred voices, we are singing. (3 times) We are not alone.

10. We are one voice, we are singing. (3 times) We are not alone.

For CDs and concert bookings contact Don at:
eatonsong@aol.com or www.small-change.org

Oh, Baha'u'llah
Bring Us Together in Unity

Greg Dahl
Used with permission

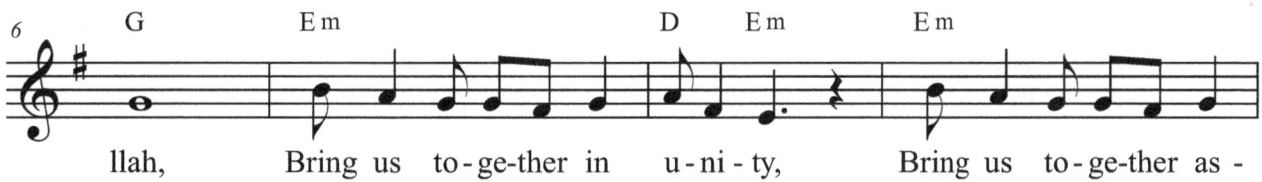
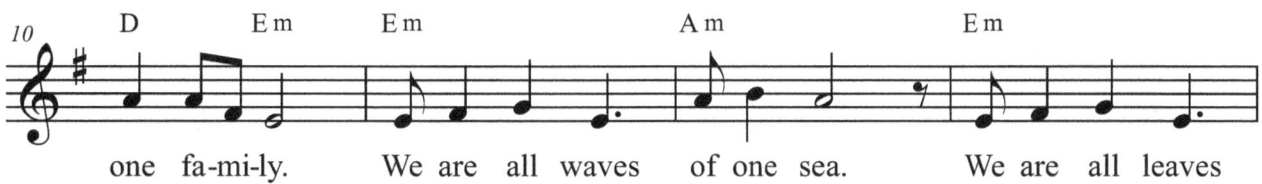

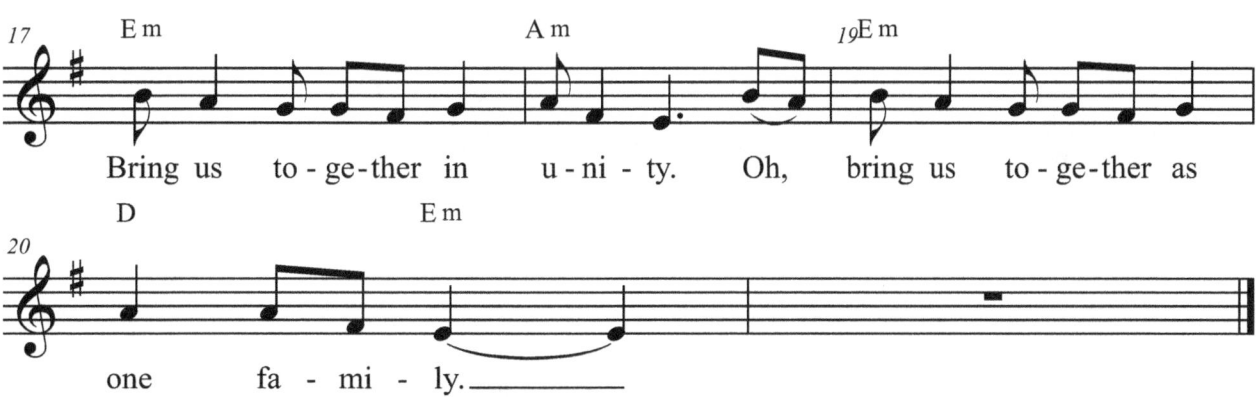

Baha'i Children's Classes and Retreats: Theme 5, p. 173

One Planet, One People, Please

Sandee English
Used with permission

One planet, one people, we all live together;
One planet, one peo— please.

1. All the world (echo) is full of people, (echo)
2. We are flowers (echo) of one garden, (echo)

And our hearts (echo) all beat as one. (echo)
We are leaves (echo) of just one tree. (echo)

Though we're different (echo) from each other, (echo)
Though we're different (echo) from each other, (echo)

We're illumined by the rays of just one sun.
We're illumined by the light of unity.

[Note: The chorus is sung in unison. The verses begin with the leader singing a phrase which is echoed by the group, until the last line of each verse which is sung in unison.]

Si Estamos Juntos

Spanish
Composer Unknown

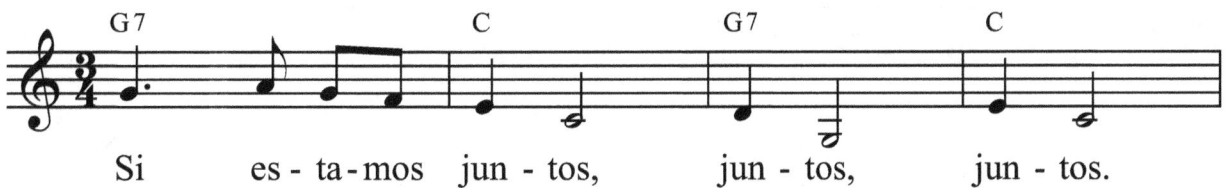
Si es-ta-mos jun-tos, jun-tos, jun-tos.

Si es-ta-mos jun-tos, me sien-to fe-liz. Tus a-

mi-gos son mi-os, Mis a-mi-gos son tu-yos.

Si es-ta-mos jun-tos me sien-to fe-liz.

What Mankind Has to Learn

Creadell Haley

We Can Build a Beautiful World

(c) Russ Garcia
Used with permission
Excerpted and simplified

(A) Green people are the best. Far better than the rest. We hate you because you're different! We are superior. You are inferior. We love us and we hate you my friend. - - -

(B) Purple people are the best. Far better than the rest. We hate you because you're different! We are superior. You are inferior. We love us and we hate you my friend.

(C) WE CAN BUILD A BEAUTIFUL WORLD, WHEN WE LEARN THAT MANKIND IS ONE. WE CAN HAVE A WONDERFUL WORLD, WHEN WE LEARN TO LOVE.

Group A sings the first verse. Group B sings the second verse. Then Group A repeats the first verse.
When they sing, "We hate you...," Group B starts again to create a round.
When Group A sings "friend" for the second time, Group C begins. Later, all join in.
(See next page for script and additional verses.)

The Power of Unity – Music

We Can Build A Beautiful World

© Russ Garcia. Music excerpted and simplified. Used with permission.

Divide children into three groups with costumes as indicated below. Include choreographed gestures if desired. The audience can also be divided into three groups, given the words, and asked to join in.

Group A: Green people are the best. Far better than the rest.
We hate you because you're different!
We are superior, you are inferior.
We love us and we hate you, my friend.

Group B: Purple people are the best. Far better than the rest.
We hate you because you're different!
We are superior, you are inferior.
We love us and we hate you, my friend.

(Sung in a round)

A: Green people are the best. Far better than the rest.
B: (silent)

A: We hate you because you're different!
B: Purple people are the best. Far better than the rest.

A: We are superior, you are inferior.
B: We hate you because you're different!

A: We love us and we hate you, my…
B: We are superior, you are inferior.

A: …friend.
B: We love us and we hate you, my…
C: WE CAN BUILD A …

A: We love us and we hate you.
B: …friend.
C: BEAUTIFUL WORLD…

A: (silent)
B: We love us and we hate you.
C: WHEN WE LEARN THAT…

A: (silent)
B: (silent)
C: MANKIND IS ONE.

Costumes

Group A: Green T-shirts
Group B: Purple T-shirts
Group C: Red or multi-colored T-shirts

Sample Gestures

For Us: Thumbs up, pat heart, thumbs in lapels

For Them: Thumbs down, press palm out, hold nose

Unifiers: Help all join hands.

All: WE CAN HAVE A WONDERFUL WORLD, WHEN WE LEARN TO LOVE.

We can build a beautiful world,
When we learn the earth is one land.
We can have a wonderful world,
When we learn to love.

We can build a beautiful world,
When we learn to love all mankind.
We can have a wonderful world,
WHEN WE LEARN TO LOVE!
LOVE!! LOVE!!! LOVE!!!! LOVE!!!!!

The Power of Unity

CLOSING ACTIVITIES

At the end of the retreat or after the final class session on this theme, the organizers may wish to plan some closing activities for the participants. We have found the following schedule to be very effective. After the cleanup, call everyone together for a celebration of their achievements.

1. **Opening:** Begin with singing and prayers.

2. **Memory quotes:** Ask for volunteers to recite any individual memory quotes learned. Then recite the main quotes together as a group, for example:

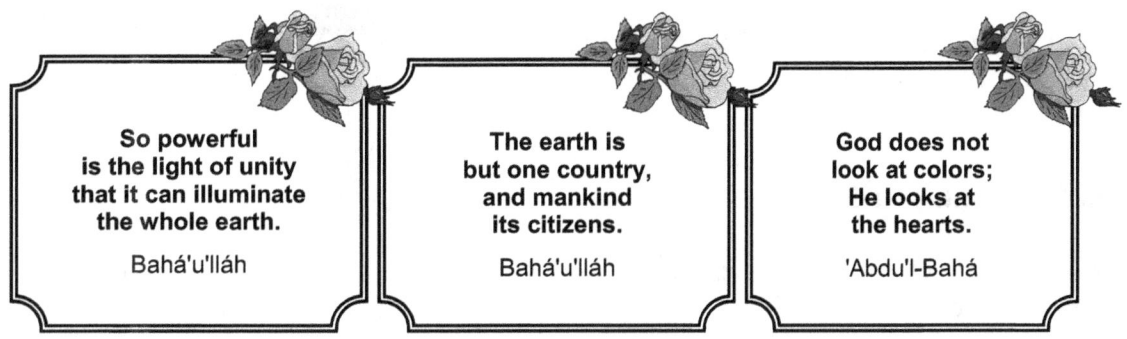

| So powerful is the light of unity that it can illuminate the whole earth. — Bahá'u'lláh | The earth is but one country, and mankind its citizens. — Bahá'u'lláh | God does not look at colors; He looks at the hearts. — 'Abdu'l-Bahá |

3. **Evaluation:** Conduct a short oral evaluation of the activities. Go around the room and ask each child, youth and adult to share brief thoughts on the three items to the right, which should be written on the board. Anyone may pass his or her turn. Suggestions can be considered in planning for the next class or retreat. An adult should take notes.

   ➢ I liked…
   ➢ I learned…
   ➢ I suggest…

4. **Appreciations:** The organizers can then share any closing comments regarding the importance of teachers (see sample quotes below) and present small gifts of appreciation to the teachers, youth volunteers, musicians, cooks and other helpers. Ask capable children to read the quotes. (The second quote usually gets a good laugh!)

> "Among the greatest of all services that can possibly be rendered by man to Almighty God is the education and training of children…It is, however, very difficult to undertake this service, even harder to succeed in it." (Selections from the Writings of 'Abdu'l-Bahá, p. 133)
>
> "If, in this momentous task, a mighty effort be exerted, the world of humanity will shine out with other adornings…The very demons will change to angels…the wild-dog pack to gazelles…and ravening beasts to peaceful herds…" (Selections from the Writings of 'Abdu'l-Bahá, p. 130)
>
> "It followeth that whatever soul shall offer his aid to bring this about will assuredly be accepted at the heavenly Threshold, and extolled by the Company on high." (Selections from the Writings of 'Abdu'l-Bahá, p. 134)
>
> "If one should, in the right way, teach and train the children, he will be performing a service than which none is greater at the Sacred Threshold." ('Abdu'l-Bahá, Bahá'í Education, p. 32)

The Power of Unity

5. **Follow-up:** Any follow-up suggestions and messages from the sponsoring Institution can be shared at this time (see next page for ideas).

6. **Graduation:** A simple ceremony (see Retreat Manual) can be held to recognize children who will be "graduating" to the Junior Youth Spiritual Empowerment Program.

7. **Announcements:** Share logistical information (lost-and-found items, rides home, etc.).

8. **Song:** Close with a sing-along, for example, "God Is One" or "Hawaiian Unity Song."

9. **Group photo:** Be sure everyone is included!

10. **Dessert:** We have a well-loved tradition of serve-yourself ice cream sundaes.

Ideas for Thank-you Gifts

As part of the closing activities, you may wish to present small thank-you gifts to the volunteers. The quote from 'Abdu'l-Bahá about universal friendship (see end of this section) makes a nice gift when photocopied onto parchment or rainbow-print paper. Additional ideas are offered below:

- Red Grammer has produced an award-winning children's recording with a variety of songs about unity and peace. To order, visit **www.redgrammer.com** and click on Store > Shop > "Teaching Peace" CD.

- UnityWorks has produced a colorful PowerPoint fireside on "The Power of Unity." Using vivid photographs, maps, demonstrations and logical proofs, this striking slide show makes a compelling statement about the oneness of humanity, the value of diversity and the need for unity. The program is available for download from **www.UnityWorksStore.com**. Click on PowerPoint Firesides.

- Special Ideas sells bumper stickers, pens, note cards, T-shirts, magnets and other items on the theme. Visit: **www.bahairesources.com** and enter "diversity" in the search box. You can also search "prejudice" for stickers and mugs, and "children of the future" for a beautiful black-and-white poster.

- The Bahá'í Media Bank offers beautiful photographs of people from around the world. The images can be downloaded and printed on cardstock or laminated. Visit **http://media.bahai.org** and click on Community.

The Power of Unity

FOLLOW-UP ACTIVITIES

Teachers and sponsoring institutions can help children apply their new knowledge and skills by providing a variety of opportunities for practice. Some examples are listed below:

- Ask the children to share during Feast what they have learned.

- Encourage them to recite memorized passages during a devotional meeting.

- Invite them to visit a class for younger children and to share one of the felt lessons about unity (*The Eye, Barriers into Bonds, The Human Body*).

- Ask them to talk about the importance of unity during a home visit.

- Encourage them to teach their friends and invite them to children's classes.

- Organize a children's fireside on "Unity in Diversity" or "Overcoming Prejudice" and have children invite their families, friends and neighbors.

- Finished craft projects can be used as teaching tools.

- Skits, demonstrations and songs from the lessons can be performed during Holy Days, Unit Convention or Cluster Reflection Meetings.

- Teachers can write a brief report on the children's class activities and submit this with photos to the local paper.

UNIVERSAL FRIENDSHIP

*What profit is there in agreeing
that universal friendship is good,
and talking of the solidarity of the human race?
...Unless these thoughts are translated
into the world of action,
they are useless.*

*When you meet a...stranger,
speak to him as to a friend;
if he seems to be lonely try to help him,
...If he be sad console him,
...if oppressed rescue him,
if in misery comfort him.
In so doing you will manifest that not in words only,
but in deed and in truth,
you think of all men as your brothers.*

*The wrong in the world continues to exist
just because people only talk of their ideals,
and do not strive to put them into practice.
If actions took the place of words,
the world's misery would very soon
be changed into comfort.*

'Abdu'l-Bahá, Paris Talks, p. 16-17

The Power of Unity

References for Teachers

Bahá'í Children's Classes and Retreats: Theme 5, p. 183

The Power of Unity

References for Teachers

LESSON #1: The Power of Unity

Unity and Love Are the Cause of Life 186
Separation Leads to Misery and Ruin 186
The Law of Attraction 186
Composition and Decomposition 187
Every Part of the Universe Is Connected 187
Bahá'u'lláh Has Proclaimed the Unity of Mankind 187
All Are Servants of One God 188
The Circle of Unity 188
Blessings and Benefits of Unity 188

LESSON #2: Unity in Diversity

Variety Lends Charm to the Garden 189
Diversity Should be the Cause of Love and Harmony 189-190
Protection of Cultural Diversity 190-191

LESSON #3: The Colors We Are

Clustered Jewels of the Races... 192
God Looks Not at Colors, but at Hearts 192
No Color Conflict in the Lower Kingdoms 192
Color Differences Due to Climate 193
All Humanity Descended from Adam and Eve 193
Unity Between Black and White 193
The Wonderful Rose Garden of Humanity 193

LESSON #4: Overcoming Prejudice

All Were Created from the Same Dust 194
Abandon Prejudices of Race 194
Consort with All People 194
Prejudices Have Caused the World's Sickness 194-195
Prejudice of Race Is Based on an Illusion 195
The Purpose of Religion Is Unity 195
Science Cannot Create Unity 195
See Ye No Strangers 195
Love the Creatures for the Sake of God 196
If You Desire Friendship with Every Race on Earth 196
The Most Vital and Challenging Issue 196

ADDITIONAL REFERENCES

Oneness of Mankind	197-198
Passages from Other Faiths	199
Leaves of One Tree	199
There Are No People of Satan; All Belong to God	199
Train the Ignorant, Heal the Sick	200
Real Unity vs. Limited Unities	200-201
Spheres of Unity	201
Prayer for Unity	202
The Principle of Oneness	202-203
World Unity the Goal	203-205
Humanity's Coming of Age	205
Role of American Bahá'ís of African Descent	206
Acceptance of Oneness Essential for Peace	206

LESSON #1

The Power of Unity

Teachers may wish to study the following references in order to gain a deeper understanding of the material presented in each lesson.

Unity and Love Are the Cause of Life

The proof is clear that in all degrees and kingdoms unity and agreement, love and fellowship are the cause of life, whereas dissension, animosity and separation are ever conducive to death.

('Abdu'l-Bahá, *Promulgation of Universal Peace,* p. 269)

Separation Leads to Misery and Ruin

Reflect ye as to other than human forms of life and be ye admonished thereby: those clouds that drift apart cannot produce the bounty of the rain, and are soon lost; a flock of sheep, once scattered, falleth prey to the wolf, and birds that fly alone will be caught fast in the claws of the hawk. What greater demonstration could there be that unity leadeth to flourishing life, while dissension and withdrawing from the others, will lead only to misery; for these are the sure ways to bitter disappointment and ruin.

('Abdu'l-Bahá, *Selections from the Writings of 'Abdu'l-Bahá,* p. 278)

The Law of Attraction

Unity is necessary to existence. Love is the very cause of life; on the other hand, separation brings death. In the world of material creation, for instance, all things owe their actual life to unity. The elements which compose wood, mineral, or stone, are held together by the law of attraction. If this law should cease for one moment to operate these elements would not hold together, they would fall apart, and the object would in that particular form cease to exist. The law of attraction has brought together certain elements in the form of this beautiful flower, but when that attraction is withdrawn from this centre the flower will decompose, and, as a flower, cease to exist.

So it is with the great body of humanity.

('Abdu'l-Bahá, *Paris Talks,* p. 138)

Composition and Decomposition

Then again, consider the phenomenon of composition and decomposition, of existence and non-existence. Every created thing in the contingent world is made up of many and varied atoms, and its existence is dependent on the composition of these. In other words, through the divine creative power a conjunction of simple elements taketh place so that from this composition a distinct organism is produced. The existence of all things is based upon this principle. But when the order is deranged, decomposition is produced and disintegration setteth in, then that thing ceaseth to exist... Therefore attraction and composition between the various elements is the means of life, and discord, decomposition and division produce death.

...Consequently, that which is conducive to association and attraction and unity among the sons of men is the means of the life of the world of humanity, and whatever causeth division, repulsion and remoteness leadeth to the death of humankind.

('Abdu'l-Bahá, *Selections from the Writings of 'Abdu'l-Bahá*, p. 289)

Every Part of the Universe Is Connected

For every part of the universe is connected with every other part by ties that are very powerful and admit of no imbalance, nor any slackening whatever. In the physical realm of creation, all things are eaters and eaten: the plant drinketh in the mineral, the animal doth crop and swallow down the plant, man doth feed upon the animal, and the mineral devoureth the body of man. Physical bodies are transferred past one barrier after another, from one life to another, and all things are subject to transformation and change, save only the essence of existence itself -- since it is constant and immutable, and upon it is founded the life of every species and kind, of every contingent reality throughout the whole of creation.

Whensoever thou dost examine, through a microscope, the water man drinketh, the air he doth breathe, thou wilt see that with every breath of air, man taketh in an abundance of animal life, and with every draught of water, he also swalloweth down a great variety of animals. How could it ever be possible to put a stop to this process? For all creatures are eaters and eaten, and the very fabric of life is reared upon this fact. Were it not so, the ties that interlace all created things within the universe would be unravelled.

('Abdu'l-Bahá, *Selections from the Writings of 'Abdu'l-Bahá*, p. 156)

Bahá'u'lláh Has Proclaimed the Unity of Mankind

Now Bahá'u'lláh has proclaimed the 'Unity of the World of Mankind'. All peoples and nations are of one family, the children of one Father, and should be to one another as brothers and sisters! I hope that you will endeavour in your lives to show forth and spread this teaching.

('Abdu'l-Bahá, *Paris Talks*, p. 140)

All Are Servants of One God

The unity which is productive of unlimited results is first a unity of mankind which recognizes that all are sheltered beneath the overshadowing glory of the All-Glorious, that all are servants of one God; for all breathe the same atmosphere, live upon the same earth, move beneath the same heavens, receive effulgence from the same sun and are under the protection of one God. This is the most great unity, and its results are lasting if humanity adheres to it; but mankind has hitherto violated it, adhering to sectarian or other limited unities such as racial, patriotic or unity of self-interests; therefore, no great results have been forthcoming....the real and ultimate unity of mankind...will bring forth marvelous results. It will reconcile all religions, make warring nations loving, cause hostile kings to become friendly and bring peace and happiness to the human world. It will cement together the Orient and Occident, remove forever the foundations of war and upraise the ensign of the Most Great Peace.

('Abdu'l-Bahá, *Promulgation of Universal Peace,* p. 191. See longer passage on p. 198)

The Circle of Unity

Bahá'u'lláh has drawn the circle of unity. He has made a design for the uniting of all the peoples, and for the gathering of them all under the shelter of the tent of universal unity. This is the work of the Divine Bounty, and we must all strive with heart and soul until we have the reality of unity in our midst, and as we work, so will strength be given unto us. Leave all thought of self, and strive only to be obedient and submissive to the Will of God. In this way only shall we become citizens of the Kingdom of God, and attain unto life everlasting.

('Abdu'l-Bahá, *Paris Talks,* p. 54)

Blessings and Benefits of Unity

How glorious the spectacle of real unity among mankind! How conducive to peace, confidence and happiness if races and nations were united in fellowship and accord! The Prophets of God were sent into the world upon this mission of unity and agreement: that these long-separated sheep might flock together...

When the racial elements of the American nation unite in actual fellowship and accord, the lights of the oneness of humanity will shine, the day of eternal glory and bliss will dawn, the spirit of God encompass, and the divine favors descend. Under the leadership and training of God, the real Shepherd, all will be protected and preserved. He will lead them in green pastures of happiness and sustenance, and they will attain to the real goal of existence. This is the blessing and benefit of unity; this is the outcome of love. This is the sign of the Most Great Peace; this is the star of the oneness of the human world.

('Abdu'l-Bahá, *Promulgation of Universal Peace,* p. 57)

LESSON #2

Unity in Diversity

Teachers may wish to study the following references in order to gain a deeper understanding of the material presented in each lesson.

Variety Lends Charm to the Garden

…the very fact that there is difference and variety lends a charm to the garden. If all were of the same color the effect would be monotonous and depressing. When you enter a rose-garden the wealth of color and variety of floral forms spread before you a picture of wonder and beauty. The world of humanity is like a garden and the various races are the flowers which constitute its adornment and decoration. In the animal kingdom also we find variety of color. See how the doves differ in beauty yet they live together in perfect peace, and love each other. They do not make difference of color a cause of discord and strife. They view each other as the same species and kind.

('Abdu'l-Bahá, *Foundations of World Unity,* p. 34)

Diversity Should Be the Cause of Love and Harmony

Behold a beautiful garden full of flowers, shrubs, and trees. Each flower has a different charm, a peculiar beauty, its own delicious perfume and beautiful colour. The trees too, how varied are they in size, in growth, in foliage—and what different fruits they bear! Yet all these flowers, shrubs and trees spring from the self-same earth, the same sun shines upon them and the same clouds give them rain.

So it is with humanity. It is made up of many races, and its peoples are of different colour, white, black, yellow, brown and red—but they all come from the same God, and all are servants to Him.

…If you beheld a garden in which all the plants were the same as to form, colour and perfume, it would not seem beautiful to you at all, but, rather, monotonous and dull…It is just the diversity and variety that constitutes its charm; each flower, each tree, each fruit, beside being beautiful in itself, brings out by contrast the qualities of the others, and shows to advantage the special loveliness of each and all.

Thus should it be among the children of men! The diversity in the human family should be the cause of love and harmony, as it is in music where many different notes blend together in the making of a perfect chord. If you meet those of different race and colour from yourself, do not mistrust them and withdraw yourself into your shell of conventionality, but rather be glad and show them kindness. Think of them as different coloured roses growing in the beautiful garden of humanity, and rejoice to be among them.

('Abdu'l-Bahá, *Paris Talks,* p. 52-53)

Protection of Cultural Diversity

...the oneness of mankind will not be based on forced assimilation, but upon protection of cultural diversity....A distinctively Bahá'í culture will welcome an infinite diversity in regard to secondary characteristics, but also firmly uphold unity in regard to fundamental principles, thereby achieving a vigorous complementarity. For example, in Selections from the Writings of 'Abdu'l-Bahá...page 260-1, we find the following intriguing statement:

What a blessing that will be—when all shall come together, even as once separate torrents, rivers and streams, running brooks and single drops, when collected together in one place will form a mighty sea. And to such a degree will the inherent unity of all prevail, that the traditions, rules, customs and distinctions in the fanciful life of these populations will be effaced and vanish away like isolated drops, once the great sea of oneness doth leap and surge and roll.

(The Universal House of Justice, *Traditional Practices in Africa,* 16 Dec 1998)

The general attitude of the Faith towards the traditional practices of various peoples is expressed in the following statement of Shoghi Effendi's, published in The World Order of Bahá'u'lláh, pages 41-42:

Let there be no misgivings as to the animating purpose of the world-wide Law of Bahá'u'lláh.... It does not ignore, nor does it attempt to suppress, the diversity of ethnical origins, of climate, of history, of language and tradition, of thought and habit, that differentiate the peoples and nations of the world.... Its watchword is unity in diversity, such as 'Abdu'l-Bahá Himself has explained:

"Consider the flowers of a garden.... Diversity of hues, form and shape enricheth and adorneth the garden, and heighteneth the effect thereof."

However, this does not mean that all traditions and practices must be preserved in a future Bahá'í society. There are certain practices which are in conflict with Bahá'í law, such as polygamy or the use of alcoholic drinks on special occasions like the birth of children, marriages, funerals and initiation ceremonies. Such practices should, obviously, be discarded, and the friends should make every effort to change their old ways and follow the way of Bahá'u'lláh.

(The Universal House of Justice, *Traditional Practices in Africa,* 16 Dec 1998)

The Power of Unity – References

Bahá'ís should obviously be encouraged to preserve their inherited cultural identities, as long as the activities involved do not contravene the principles of the Faith. The perpetuation of such cultural characteristics is an expression of unity in diversity.

(On behalf of the Universal House of Justice, 26 May 1982, *Lights of Guidance,* p. 553)

The Bahá'í Faith seeks to maintain cultural diversity while promoting the unity of all peoples. Indeed, such diversity will enrich the tapestry of human life in a peaceful world society. The House of Justice supports the view that in every country it is quite appropriate for the cultural traditions of the people to be observed within the Bahá'í community as long as they are not contrary to the teachings....At the present time, the challenge to every Bahá'í community is to avoid suppression of those culturally-diverse elements which are not contrary to the teachings, while establishing and maintaining such a high degree of unity that others are attracted to the Cause of God.

(On behalf of the Universal House of Justice, 25 July 1988,
www.bci.org/nnby/principals/protection_of_cultural_diversity.htm)

LESSON #3

The Colors We Are

Teachers may wish to study the following references in order to gain a deeper understanding of the material presented in each lesson.

Clustered Jewels of the Races

In the clustered jewels of the races may the blacks be as sapphires and rubies and the whites as diamonds and pearls. The composite beauty of humanity will be witnessed in their unity and blending. How glorious the spectacle of real unity among mankind!

('Abdu'l-Bahá, *Promulgation of Universal Peace,* p. 57)

God Looks Not at Colors, but at Hearts

In the estimation of God there is no distinction of color; all are one in the color and beauty of servitude to Him. Color is not important; the heart is all-important…God does not behold differences of hue and complexion; He looks at the hearts. He whose morals and virtues are praiseworthy is preferred in the presence of God; he who is devoted to the Kingdom is most beloved.

('Abdu'l-Bahá, *Foundations of World Unity,* p. 34)

No Color Conflict in the Lower Kingdoms

The mineral kingdom abounds with many-colored substances…but we find no strife among them on that account. In the kingdom of the plant and vegetable, distinct…hues exist but the fruit and flowers are not in conflict for that reason…Throughout the animal kingdom we do not find the creatures separated because of color. They recognize unity of species and oneness of kind. If we do not find color distinction drawn in a kingdom of lower intelligence and reason, how can it be justified among human beings…?

('Abdu'l-Bahá, *Foundations of World Unity,* p. 34)

Now ponder this: Animals, despite the fact that they lack reason and understanding, do not make colors the cause of conflict. Why should man, who has reason, create conflict? This is wholly unworthy of him.

('Abdu'l-Bahá, *Promulgation of Universal Peace,* p. 45)

Color Differences Due to Climate

Indeed, the world of humanity is like one kindred and one family. Because of the climatic differences of the zones, through the passing of ages colors have become different. In the torrid zone, on account of the intensity of the effect of the sun throughout the ages the black race appeared. In the frigid zone, on account of the severity of the cold and the ineffectiveness of the heat of the sun throughout the ages the white race appeared. In the temperate zone, the yellow, brown and red races came into existence. But in reality mankind is one race.

('Abdu'l-Bahá, *The Power of Unity,* p. 48)

All Humanity Descended from Adam and Eve

Adam was of one color. Eve had one color. All humanity is descended from them. Therefore, in origin they are one. These colors developed later due to climates and regions; they have no significance whatsoever.

('Abdu'l-Bahá, *Promulgation of Universal Peace,* p. 45)

Unity Between Black and White

There is no sheep which shuns another as if saying, "I am white, and you are black." They graze together in complete unity…How then can man be limited and influenced by racial colors?

('Abdu'l-Bahá, *Promulgation of Universal Peace,* p. 425)

Therefore today I am exceedingly glad that both white and colored people have gathered here and I hope the time will come when they shall live together in the utmost peace, unity and friendship.…I pray in your behalf that there shall be no name other than that of humanity among you.
…For the accomplishment of unity between the colored and whites will be an assurance of the world's peace.

('Abdu'l-Bahá, *Foundations of World Unity,* p. 34-35)

See also: Shoghi Effendi's selection of quotations in *Advent of Divine Justice,* p. 36-41

The Wonderful Rose Garden of Humanity

I hope you will continue in unity and fellowship. How beautiful to see blacks and whites together! I hope, God willing, the day may come when I shall see the red men, the Indians, with you, also Japanese and others. Then there will be white roses, yellow roses, red roses, and a very wonderful rose garden will appear in the world.

('Abdu'l-Bahá, *Promulgation of Universal Peace,* p. 428)

The Power of Unity – References

LESSON #4

Overcoming Prejudice

Teachers may wish to study the following references in order to gain a deeper understanding of the material presented in each lesson.

All Were Created from the Same Dust

O CHILDREN OF MEN! Know ye not why We created you all from the same dust? That no one should exalt himself over the other. Ponder at all times in your hearts how ye were created. Since We have created you all from one same substance it is incumbent on you to be even as one soul, to walk with the same feet, eat with the same mouth and dwell in the same land, that from your inmost being, by your deeds and actions, the signs of oneness and the essence of detachment may be made manifest. Such is My counsel to you, O concourse of light! Heed ye this counsel that ye may obtain the fruit of holiness from the tree of wondrous glory.

(Bahá'u'lláh, *Arabic Hidden Words*, #68)

Abandon Prejudices of Race

O humankind! Verily, ye are all the leaves and fruits of one tree; ye are all one. Therefore, associate in friendship; love one another; abandon prejudices of race…For thousands of years ye have been contending in warfare and strife. It is enough. Now is the time for unity.

('Abdu'l-Bahá, quoting Bahá'u'lláh, *Promulgation of Universal Peace,* p. 322)

Consort with All People

Consort with all the people in love and fragrance. Fellowship is the cause of unity, and unity is the source of order in the world. Blessed are they who are kind and serve with love.

(Bahá'u'lláh, *Bahá'í Scriptures,* p. 157)

Prejudices Have Caused the World's Sickness

All prejudices, whether of religion, race, politics or nation, must be renounced, for these prejudices have caused the world's sickness. It is a grave malady which, unless arrested, is capable of causing the destruction of the whole human race. Every ruinous war, with its terrible bloodshed and misery, has been caused by one or other of these prejudices.

...Until all these barriers erected by prejudice are swept away, it is not possible for humanity to be at peace.

('Abdu'l-Bahá, *Paris Talks,* p. 146-147)

Prejudice of Race Is Based on an Illusion

Concerning prejudice of race: it is an illusion, a superstition pure and simple! For God created us all of one race.... In the sight of God there is no difference between the various races. Why should man invent such a prejudice?

...The only difference lies in the degree of faithfulness, of obedience to the laws of God. There are some who are as lighted torches, there are others who shine as stars in the sky of humanity. The lovers of mankind, these are the superior men, of whatever nation, creed, or colour they may be.

.....On the other hand there are those selfish men, haters of their brethren, in whose hearts prejudice has replaced loving kindness, and whose influence breeds discord and strife.

('Abdu'l-Bahá, *Paris Talks,* p. 148-149)

The Purpose of Religion Is Unity

The essential purpose of the religion of God is to establish unity among mankind.

('Abdu'l-Bahá, *Promulgation of Universal Peace,* p. 202)

Science Cannot Create Unity

Science cannot create amity and fellowship in human hearts. Neither can patriotism or racial allegiance effect a remedy...The spiritual teachings of the religion of God can alone create this love...

('Abdu'l-Bahá, *Divine Art of Living,* p. 112-113)

See Ye No Strangers

See ye no strangers; rather see all men as friends... For each of the creatures is a sign of God, and it was by the grace of the Lord and His power that each did step into the world; therefore they are not strangers, but in the family; not aliens, but friends, and to be treated as such.

('Abdu'l-Bahá, *Selections from the Writings of 'Abdu'l-Bahá,* p. 24)

Love the Creatures for the Sake of God

Be in perfect unity. Never become angry with one another....Love the creatures for the sake of God...There are imperfections in every human being, and you will always become unhappy if you look toward the people themselves...You must love and be kind to everybody, care for the poor, protect the weak, heal the sick, teach and educate the ignorant.

('Abdu'l-Bahá, *Promulgation of Universal Peace,* p. 92)

If You Desire Friendship with Every Race on Earth

If you desire with all your heart friendship with every race on earth, your thought will spread; it will become the desire of others, growing stronger and stronger, until it reaches the minds of all men.

('Abdu'l-Bahá, *Divine Art of Living,* p. 111)

The Most Vital and Challenging Issue

As to racial prejudice, the corrosion of which, for well-nigh a century, has bitten into the fiber, and attacked the whole social structure of American society, it should be regarded as constituting the most vital and challenging issue confronting the Bahá'í community at the present stage of its evolution. The ceaseless exertions which this issue of paramount importance calls for, the sacrifices it must impose, the care and vigilance it demands, the moral courage and fortitude it requires, the tact and sympathy it necessitates, invest this problem, which the American believers are still far from having satisfactorily resolved, with an urgency and importance that cannot be overestimated.

(Shoghi Effendi, *Advent of Divine Justice,* p. 33-34. See p. 33-41 for complete passage.)

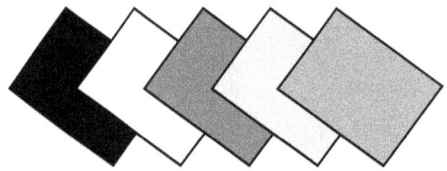

ADDITIONAL REFERENCES ON UNITY

All teachers may wish to study the following references.

Oneness of Mankind

In the Bahá'í Writings, the oneness of mankind has been referred to as:

- The foundation of the Faith of God (See reference #1, below.)
- The distinguishing feature of His Law (#1)
- Bahá'u'lláh's supreme declaration (#2)
- The chief and distinguishing feature of the Faith (#2)
- The pivot round which all the teachings of Bahá'u'lláh revolve (#3)
- The consummation of human evolution (#4)
- The head corner-stone of Bahá'u'lláh's all-embracing dominion (#5)
- A warning and a promise (#5)
- The sole means for the salvation of a greatly suffering world (#5)
- The cornerstone of the Religion of God (#6)
- The cornerstone of all the teachings of Bahá'u'lláh (#7)
- The cardinal principle of the Faith (#8)
- The operating principle and ultimate goal of His Revelation (#9)
- The principal mission of Bahá'u'lláh (#10)
- A spiritual truth which all the human sciences confirm (#11)

References

1. "In every Dispensation," writes 'Abdu'l-Bahá, "the light of Divine Guidance has been focussed upon one central theme.... In this wondrous Revelation, this glorious century, the foundation of the Faith of God and the distinguishing feature of His Law is the consciousness of the Oneness of Mankind." ('Abdu'l-Bahá, quoted in Shoghi Effendi, *World Order of Bahá'u'lláh*, p. 36)

2. Are not these intermittent crises that convulse present-day society due primarily to the lamentable inability of the world's recognized leaders to read aright the signs of the times, to rid themselves once for all of their preconceived ideas and fettering creeds, and to reshape the machinery of their respective governments according to those standards that are implicit in Bahá'u'lláh's supreme declaration of the Oneness of Mankind—the chief and distinguishing feature of the Faith He proclaimed? (Shoghi Effendi, *World Order of Bahá'u'lláh*, p. 36)

The Power of Unity – References

3. Let there be no mistake. The principle of the Oneness of Mankind—the pivot round which all the teachings of Bahá'u'lláh revolve—is no mere outburst of ignorant emotionalism or an expression of vague and pious hope. (Shoghi Effendi, *World Order of Bahá'u'lláh*, p. 42)

4. It represents the consummation of human evolution—an evolution that has had its earliest beginnings in the birth of family life, its subsequent development in the achievement of tribal solidarity, leading in turn to the constitution of the city-state, and expanding later into the institution of independent and sovereign nations. (Shoghi Effendi, *World Order of Bahá'u'lláh*, p. 43. See longer passage on p. 200-201)

5. The proclamation of the Oneness of Mankind—the head corner-stone of Bahá'u'lláh's all-embracing dominion—can under no circumstances be compared with such expressions of pious hope as have been uttered in the past… It implies at once a warning and a promise—a warning that in it lies the sole means for the salvation of a greatly suffering world, a promise that its realization is at hand. (Shoghi Effendi, *World Order of Bahá'u'lláh*, p. 46)

6. To the faithful followers of Bahá'u'lláh who fully grasp the essential implications of the principle of the oneness of mankind so much emphasized in His teachings, racial prejudice, in all its forms, is simply a negation of faith, a repudiation, of the belief in the brotherhood of man which is beyond doubt, the corner-stone of the Religion of God. (On behalf of Shoghi Effendi, *Lights of Guidance*, p. 531)

7. …the principle of the oneness of humanity is the corner-stone of all the teachings of Bahá'u'lláh. (On behalf of Shoghi Effendi, *Lights of Guidance*, p. 506)

8. The friends must remember that the cardinal principle of their Faith is the Oneness of Mankind. (On behalf of Shoghi Effendi, *Lights of Guidance*, p. 524)

9. The oneness of mankind, which is at once the operating principle and ultimate goal of His Revelation, implies the achievement of a dynamic coherence between the spiritual and practical requirements of life on earth. (The Universal House of Justice, *Lights of Guidance*, p. 544)

10. Bahá'u'lláh's principal mission in appearing at this time in human history is the realization of the oneness of mankind and the establishment of peace among the nations… (On behalf of the Universal House of Justice, *Lights of Guidance*, p. 436)

11. World order can be founded only on an unshakable consciousness of the oneness of mankind, a spiritual truth which all the human sciences confirm. (The Universal House of Justice, *The Promise of World Peace*, p. 4)

The Power of Unity – References

Passages from Other Faiths

- **Hinduism:** Be united in your purpose, let your hearts be as one heart… (Rig Veda 8:7)
- **Buddhism:** So what of all these titles, names, and races? They are mere worldly conventions. (Sutta Nipata 648)
- **Judaism:** Have we not all one father? Hath not one God created us? (Malachi 2:10)
- **Christianity:** God…hath made of one blood all nations of men for to dwell on all the face of the earth. (Acts 17:26)
- **Islam**: O mankind! We created you from a single pair of a male and a female and made you into nations and tribes. (Qur'an 49.13)

Leaves of One Tree

A fundamental teaching of Bahá'u'lláh is the oneness of the world of humanity. Addressing mankind, He says, "Ye are all leaves of one tree and the fruits of one branch." By this it is meant that the world of humanity is like a tree, the nations or peoples are the different limbs or branches of that tree, and the individual human creatures are as the fruits and blossoms thereof. In this way Bahá'u'lláh expressed the oneness of humankind, whereas in all religious teachings of the past the human world has been represented as divided into two parts: one known as the people of the Book of God, or the pure tree, and the other the people of infidelity and error, or the evil tree. The former were considered as belonging to the faithful, and the others to the hosts of the irreligious and infidel—one part of humanity the recipients of divine mercy, and the other the object of the wrath of their Creator. Bahá'u'lláh removed this by proclaiming the oneness of the world of humanity, and this principle is specialized in His teachings, for He has submerged all mankind in the sea of divine generosity. Some are asleep; they need to be awakened. Some are ailing; they need to be healed. Some are immature as children; they need to be trained. But all are recipients of the bounty and bestowals of God.

('Abdu'l-Bahá, *Promulgation of Universal Peace,* p. 454)

There Are No People of Satan; All Belong to God

When the light of Bahá'u'lláh dawned from the East, He proclaimed the promise of the oneness of humanity. He addressed all mankind, saying, "Ye are all the fruits of one tree. There are not two trees: one a tree of divine mercy, the other the tree of Satan." …He said, "It is not becoming in man to curse another; it is not befitting that man should attribute darkness to another; it is not meet that one human being should consider another human being as bad; nay, rather, all mankind are the servants of one God; God is the Father of all; there is not a single exception to that law. There are no people of Satan; all belong to the Merciful. There is no darkness; all is light."

('Abdu'l-Bahá, *Promulgation of Universal Peace,* p. 266)

Train the Ignorant, Heal the Sick

...among mankind there may be those who are ignorant; they must be trained. Some are sick; they must be treated. Some are immature; they must be helped to attain maturity....Just as God loves all and is kind to all, so must we really love and be kind to everybody. We must consider none bad, none worthy of detestation, no one as an enemy. We must love all; nay, we must consider everyone as related to us, for all are the servants of one God.

('Abdu'l-Bahá, *Promulgation of Universal Peace*, p. 267)

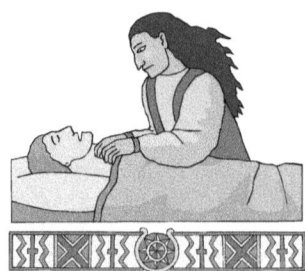

God is kind to all. Mankind are His sheep, and He is their real Shepherd. No other scriptures contain such breadth and universality of statement; no other teachings proclaim this unequivocal principle of the solidarity of humanity. As regards any possible distinctions, the utmost that Bahá'u'lláh says is that conditions among men vary, that some, for instance, are defective.

Therefore, such souls must be educated in order that they may be brought to the degree of perfection. Some are sick and ailing; they must be treated and cared for until they are healed. Some are asleep; they need to be awakened. Some are immature as children; they should be helped to attain maturity. But all must be loved and cherished. The child must not be disliked simply because it is a child. Nay, rather, it should be patiently educated. The sick one must not be avoided nor slighted merely because he is ailing. Nay, rather, he must be regarded with sympathy and affection and treated until he is healed. The soul that is asleep must not be looked upon with contempt but awakened and led into the light.

('Abdu'l-Bahá, *Promulgation of Universal Peace*, p. 433-434)

Real Unity vs. Limited Unities

The unity which is productive of unlimited results is first a unity of mankind which recognizes that all are sheltered beneath the overshadowing glory of the All-Glorious; that all are servants of one God; for all breathe the same atmosphere, live upon the same earth, move beneath the same heavens, receive effulgence from the same sun and are under the protection of one God. This is the most great unity, and its results are lasting if humanity adheres to it; but mankind has hitherto violated it, adhering to sectarian or other limited unities such as racial, patriotic or unity of self-interests; therefore no great results have been forthcoming. Nevertheless...capacity exists for the proclamation and promulgation of the real and ultimate unity of mankind which will bring forth marvelous results. It will reconcile all religions, make warring nations loving, cause hostile kings to become friendly and bring peace and happiness to the human world. It will cement together the Orient and Occident, remove forever the foundations of war and upraise the ensign of the "Most Great Peace". These limited unities are therefore signs of that great unity which will make all the human family one...

The Power of Unity – References

Another unity is the spiritual unity which emanates from the breaths of the Holy Spirit. This is greater than the unity of mankind. Human unity or solidarity may be likened to the body whereas unity from the breaths of the Holy Spirit is the spirit animating the body. This is a perfect unity. It creates such a condition in mankind that each one will make sacrifices for the other and the utmost desire will be to forfeit life and all that pertains to it in behalf of another's good. This is the unity which existed among the disciples of His Holiness Jesus Christ and bound together the prophets and holy souls of the past…This unity is the very spirit of the body of the world.

…In the Word of God there is still another unity, the oneness of the Manifestations of God, His Holiness Abraham, Moses, Jesus Christ, Mohammed, the Báb and Bahá'u'lláh. This is a unity divine, heavenly, radiant, merciful; the one reality appearing in its successive manifestations. …Although these dawning-points are different, the sun is the same sun which has appeared from them all.

…There is also the divine unity or entity which is sanctified above all concept of humanity. It cannot be comprehended nor conceived because it is infinite reality and cannot become finite. Human minds are incapable of surrounding that reality…This is the unity of God; this is oneness;—unity of divinity, holy above ascent or descent, embodiment, comprehension or idealization; —divine unity—the prophets are its mirrors; its lights are revealed through them; its virtues become resplendent in them, but the Sun of Reality never descends from its own highest point and station. This is unity, oneness, sanctity; this is glorification whereby we praise and adore God.

('Abdu'l-Bahá, *Foundations of World Unity*, p. 66-68)

Spheres of Unity

Note ye how easily, where unity existeth in a given family, the affairs of that family are conducted; what progress the members of that family make, how they prosper in the world. Their concerns are in order, they enjoy comfort and tranquillity, they are secure, their position is assured, they come to be envied by all. Such a family but addeth to its stature and its lasting honour, as day succeedeth day. And if we widen out the sphere of unity a little to include the inhabitants of a village who seek to be loving and united, who associate with and are kind to one another, what great advances they will be seen to make, how secure and protected they will be. Then let us widen out the sphere a little more, let us take the inhabitants of a city, all of them together: if they establish the strongest bonds of unity among themselves, how far they will progress, even in a brief period and what power they will exert. And if the sphere of unity be still further widened out, that is, if the inhabitants of a whole country develop peaceable hearts, and if with all their hearts and souls they yearn to cooperate with one another and to live in unity, and if they become kind and loving to one another, that country will achieve undying joy and lasting glory. Peace will it have, and plenty, and vast wealth.

('Abdu'l-Bahá, *Selections from the Writings of 'Abdu'l-Bahá*, p. 279)

Prayer for Unity

O Thou kind Lord! Thou hast created all humanity from the same stock. Thou hast decreed that all shall belong to the same household. In Thy Holy Presence they are all Thy servants, and all mankind are sheltered beneath Thy Tabernacle; all have gathered together at Thy Table of Bounty; all are illumined through the light of Thy Providence.

O God! Thou art kind to all, Thou hast provided for all, dost shelter all, conferrest life upon all. Thou hast endowed each and all with talents and faculties, and all are submerged in the Ocean of Thy Mercy.

O Thou kind Lord! Unite all. Let the religions agree and make the nations one, so that they may see each other as one family and the whole earth as one home. May they all live together in perfect harmony.

O God! Raise aloft the banner of the oneness of mankind.

O God! Establish the Most Great Peace.

Cement Thou, O God, the hearts together.

O Thou kind Father, God! Gladden our hearts through the fragrance of Thy love. Brighten our eyes through the Light of Thy Guidance. Delight our ears with the melody of Thy Word, and shelter us all in the Stronghold of Thy Providence.

Thou art the Mighty and Powerful, Thou art the Forgiving and Thou art the One Who overlooketh the shortcomings of all mankind.

('Abdu'l-Bahá, *Promulgation of Universal Peace,* p. 100-101)

The Principle of Oneness

Let there be no mistake. The principle of the Oneness of Mankind—the pivot round which all the teachings of Bahá'u'lláh revolve—is no mere outburst of ignorant emotionalism or an expression of vague and pious hope. Its appeal is not to be merely identified with a reawakening of the spirit of brotherhood and good-will among men, nor does it aim solely at the fostering of harmonious cooperation among individual peoples and nations. Its implications are deeper, its claims greater than any which the Prophets of old were allowed to advance. Its message is applicable not only to the individual, but concerns itself primarily with the nature of those essential relationships that must bind all the states and nations as members of one human family. It does not constitute merely the enunciation of an ideal, but stands inseparably associated with an institution adequate to embody its truth, demonstrate its validity, and perpetuate its influence. It implies an organic change in the structure of present-day society, a change such as the world has not yet experienced. It constitutes a challenge, at once bold and universal, to outworn shibboleths of national creeds—creeds that have had their day and which must, in the ordinary course of events as shaped and controlled by Providence, give way to a new gospel, fundamentally different from, and infinitely superior to, what the world has already conceived. It calls for no less than the reconstruction and the demilitarization of the whole civilized world—a world organically unified in all the essential aspects of its life, its political machinery, its spiritual aspiration, its trade and finance, its script and language, and yet infinite in the diversity of the national characteristics of its federated units.

It represents the consummation of human evolution—an evolution that has had its earliest beginnings in the birth of family life, its subsequent development in the achievement of tribal solidarity, leading in turn to the constitution of the city-state, and expanding later into the institution of independent and sovereign nations.

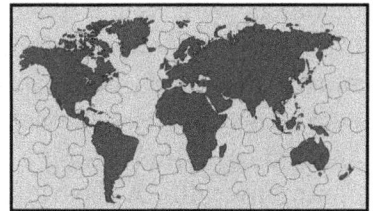

The principle of the Oneness of Mankind, as proclaimed by Bahá'u'lláh, carries with it no more and no less than a solemn assertion that attainment to this final stage in this stupendous evolution is not only necessary but inevitable, that its realization is fast approaching, and that nothing short of a power that is born of God can succeed in establishing it.

(Shoghi Effendi, *World Order of Bahá'u'lláh,* p. 42)

World Unity the Goal

Unification of the whole of mankind is the hall-mark of the stage which human society is now approaching. Unity of family, of tribe, of city-state, and nation have been successively attempted and fully established. World unity is the goal towards which a harassed humanity is striving. Nation-building has come to an end. The anarchy inherent in state sovereignty is moving towards a climax. A world, growing to maturity, must abandon this fetish, recognize the oneness and wholeness of human relationships, and establish once for all the machinery that can best incarnate this fundamental principle of its life.

"A new life," Bahá'u'lláh proclaims, "is, in this age, stirring within all the peoples of the earth; and yet none hath discovered its cause, or perceived its motive." "O ye children of men," He thus addresses His generation, "the fundamental purpose animating the Faith of God and His Religion is to safeguard the interests and promote the unity of the human race... This is the straight path, the fixed and immovable foundation. Whatsoever is raised on this foundation, the changes and chances of the world can never impair its strength, nor will the revolution of countless centuries undermine its structure." "The well-being of mankind," He declares, "its peace and security are unattainable unless and until its unity is firmly established." "So powerful is the light of unity," is His further testimony, "that it can illuminate the whole earth. The one true God, He Who knoweth all things, Himself testifieth to the truth of these words... This goal excelleth every other goal, and this aspiration is the monarch of all aspirations." "He Who is your Lord, the All-Merciful," He, moreover, has written, "cherisheth in His heart the desire of beholding the entire human race as one soul and one body. Haste ye to win your share of God's good grace and mercy in this Day that eclipseth all other created days."

The Power of Unity – References

The unity of the human race, as envisaged by Bahá'u'lláh, implies the establishment of a world commonwealth in which all nations, races, creeds and classes are closely and permanently united, and in which the autonomy of its state members and the personal freedom and initiative of the individuals that compose them are definitely and completely safeguarded. This commonwealth must, as far as we can visualize it, consist of a world legislature, whose members will, as the trustees of the whole of mankind, ultimately control the entire resources of all the component nations, and will enact such laws as shall be required to regulate the life, satisfy the needs and adjust the relationships of all races and peoples. A world executive, backed by an international Force, will carry out the decisions arrived at, and apply the laws enacted by, this world legislature, and will safeguard the organic unity of the whole commonwealth. A world tribunal will adjudicate and deliver its compulsory and final verdict in all and any disputes that may arise between the various elements constituting this universal system. A mechanism of world inter-communication will be devised, embracing the whole planet, freed from national hindrances and restrictions, and functioning with marvellous swiftness and perfect regularity. A world metropolis will act as the nerve center of a world civilization, the focus towards which the unifying forces of life will converge and from which its energizing influences will radiate. A world language will either be invented or chosen from among the existing languages and will be taught in the schools of all the federated nations as an auxiliary to their mother tongue. A world script, a world literature, a uniform and universal system of currency, of weights and measures, will simplify and facilitate intercourse and understanding among the nations and races of mankind. In such a world society, science and religion, the two most potent forces in human life, will be reconciled, will cooperate, and will harmoniously develop. The press will, under such a system, while giving full scope to the expression of the diversified views and convictions of mankind, cease to be mischievously manipulated by vested interests, whether private or public, and will be liberated from the influence of contending governments and peoples. The economic resources of the world will be organized, its sources of raw materials will be tapped and fully utilized, its markets will be coordinated and developed, and the distribution of its products will be equitably regulated.

National rivalries, hatreds, and intrigues will cease, and racial animosity and prejudice will be replaced by racial amity, understanding and cooperation. The causes of religious strife will be permanently removed, economic barriers and restrictions will be completely abolished, and the inordinate distinction between classes will be obliterated. Destitution on the one hand, and gross accumulation of ownership on the other, will disappear. The enormous energy dissipated and wasted on war, whether economic or political, will be consecrated to such ends as will  extend the range of human inventions and technical development, to the increase of the productivity of mankind, to the extermination of disease, to the extension of scientific research, to the raising of the standard of physical health, to the sharpening and refinement of the human brain, to the exploitation of the unused and unsuspected resources of the planet, to the prolongation of human life, and to the furtherance of any other agency that can stimulate the intellectual, the moral, and spiritual life of the entire human race.

The Power of Unity – References

A world federal system, ruling the whole earth and exercising unchallengeable authority over its unimaginably vast resources, blending and embodying the ideals of both the East and the West, liberated from the curse of war and its miseries, and bent on the exploitation of all the available sources of energy on the surface of the planet, a system in which Force is made the servant of Justice, whose life is sustained by its universal recognition of one God and by its allegiance to one common Revelation—such is the goal towards which humanity, impelled by the unifying forces of life, is moving.

"One of the great events," affirms 'Abdu'l-Bahá, "which is to occur in the Day of the manifestation of that incomparable Branch is the hoisting of the Standard of God among all nations. By this is meant that all nations and kindreds will be gathered together under the shadow of this Divine Banner, which is no other than the Lordly Branch itself, and will become a single nation. Religious and sectarian antagonism, the hostility of races and peoples, and differences among nations, will be eliminated. All men will adhere to one religion, will have one common faith, will be blended into one race and become a single people. All will dwell in one common fatherland, which is the planet itself." "Now, in the world of being," He has moreover explained, "the Hand of Divine power hath firmly laid the foundations of this all-highest bounty, and this wondrous gift. Whatsoever is latent in the innermost of this holy Cycle shall gradually appear and be made manifest, for now is but the beginning of its growth, and the dayspring of the revelation of its signs. Ere the close of this century and of this age, it shall be made clear and evident how wondrous was that spring-tide, and how heavenly was that gift."

(Shoghi Effendi, *World Order of Bahá'u'lláh*, p. 202 -205)

Humanity's Coming of Age

The Revelation of Bahá'u'lláh, whose supreme mission is none other but the achievement of this organic and spiritual unity of the whole body of nations, should, if we be faithful to its implications, be regarded as signalizing through its advent the coming of age of the entire human race. It should be viewed not merely as yet another spiritual revival in the ever-changing fortunes of mankind, not only as a further stage in a chain of progressive Revelations, nor even as the culmination of one of a series of recurrent prophetic cycles, but rather as marking the last and highest stage in the stupendous evolution of man's collective life on this planet. The emergence of a world community, the consciousness of world citizenship, the founding of a world civilization and culture… should, by their very nature, be regarded, as far as this planetary life is concerned, as the furthermost limits in the organization of human society…

(Shoghi Effendi, *World Order of Baha'u'llah,* p. 163)

The Power of Unity – References

Role of American Bahá'ís of African Descent

It is always important to remember that with the coming of Bahá'u'lláh the human race as a whole was summoned to recognition of its oneness, and this has launched it on a wholly new stage in its spiritual and social evolution. He has stated clearly that His message and the glorious prospects envisaged belong to every people on the planet. "The summons and the message," He wrote, "which We gave were never intended to reach or to benefit one land or one people only. Mankind in its entirety must firmly adhere to whatsoever hath been revealed and vouchsafed unto it. Then and only then will it attain unto true liberty."

Yet, it is clear, too, from the Teachings that every people, through its inherent potentialities and particular range of experience, will make its own distinct contribution to the creation of a new civilization. To the extent that African-Americans who embrace the new Revelation arise to do their part by adhering to the Teachings will the gifts which are uniquely theirs be realized in the splendors of the Golden Age. The "pupil of the eye," Bahá'u'lláh's metaphoric reference to Black people, will no doubt acquire clear meaning as they conscientiously strive over time to fulfill the divine purpose for which the Blessed Beauty came. There can be no doubt that Americans of African descent can find in themselves the capacity, so well developed as a result of their long encounter with injustice, to recognize and respond to the vision of love and justice brought by the Promised One of all ages. Imbued with that vision, past and present sufferings are transformed into measures of patience, wisdom and compassion—qualities so essential to the effort to moderate the discordant ways of a confused world and aid the healing of its spiritual ills. What better than the transformed character of a bruised people to smooth the course, to offer perspectives for new beginnings toward world order!

(The Universal House of Justice, letter to an individual, 3 June 2007)

> Complete document available on the Bahá'í administrative website: < www.usbnc.org >.
> Click on: Communications > Universal House of Justice > 2007, and scroll down to June 3.
>
> See also: *Pupil of the Eye: African Americans in the World Order of Bahá'u'lláh.* Selections from the Bahá'í Writings, compiled by Bonnie J. Taylor. < http://bahai-library.com/?file=taylor_pupil_eye >.

Acceptance of Oneness Essential for Peace

World order can be founded only on an unshakable consciousness of the oneness of mankind, a spiritual truth which all the human sciences confirm. Anthropology, physiology, psychology, recognize only one human species, albeit infinitely varied in the secondary aspects of life. Recognition of this truth requires abandonment of prejudice—prejudice of every kind—race, class, colour, creed, nation, sex, degree of material civilization, everything which enables people to consider themselves superior to others.

Acceptance of the oneness of mankind is the first fundamental prerequisite for reorganization and administration of the world as one country, the home of humankind. Universal acceptance of this spiritual principle is essential to any successful attempt to establish world peace....

(The Universal House of Justice, *The Promise of World Peace,* October 1985)

BIBLIOGRAPHY

Advent of Divine Justice. Shoghi Effendi. Bahá'í Publishing Trust: Wilmette, Illinois, 1971.

All the Colors We Are. Todos los Colores de Nuestra Piel: The Story of How We Get Our Skin Color. Katie Kissinger and Wernher Krutein. Redleaf Press: Minnesota, 1994.

Bahá'í Education: A Compilation. Compiled by the Research Department of the Universal House of Justice. Bahá'í Publishing Trust: Wilmette, Illinois, 1978.

Bahá'í Prayers. A Selection of Prayers Revealed by Bahá'u'lláh, The Báb and 'Abdu'l-Bahá. Bahá'í Publishing Trust: Wilmette, Illinois, 1954, 1991 edition.

Bahá'í Public Speaking: Teacher's Guide with Nine Workshops for Children, Youth and Adults. Randie Gottlieb. UnityWorks: Yakima, Washington, 2001, revised 2007.

Bahá'í Scriptures: Selections from the Utterances of Bahá'u'lláh and 'Abdu'l-Bahá. Horace Holley, ed. Bahá'í Publishing Committee: New York, 1928 edition.

Because We Can Change the World: A Practical Guide to Building Cooperative, Inclusive Classroom Communities. Mara Sapon-Shevin. Allyn and Bacon: Boston, 1999.

Building Bridges: A Bahá'í Songbook. Compiled and prepared by Peggy Caton and Dale Nomura under the direction of the Bahá'í National Education Committee. Kalimát Press: Los Angeles, 1984.

Developing Distinctive Bahá'í Communities: Guidelines for Spiritual Assemblies. Office of Assembly Development, National Spiritual Assembly of the Bahá'ís of the United States: Evanston, Illinois, 1998.

The Divine Art of Living, Selections from Writings of Bahá'u'lláh and 'Abdu'l-Bahá. Compiled by Mabel Hyde Paine, revised by Anne Marie Scheffer. Bahá'í Publishing Trust: Wilmette, Illinois, revised edition 1986.

The Elimination of Prejudice. Star Study Program. Bahá'í Publishing Trust, Wilmette, Illinois, 1975.

Foundations of World Unity. 'Abdu'l-Bahá. Bahá'í Publishing Trust: Wilmette, Illinois, 1945, fourth printing 1968.

Gleanings from the Writings of Bahá'u'lláh. Bahá'u'lláh. Translated by Shoghi Effendi. Bahá'í Publishing Trust: Wilmette, Illinois, 1952, 1983 edition.

The Hidden Words. Bahá'u'lláh. Translated by Shoghi Effendi with the assistance of some English friends. Bahá'í Publishing Trust: Wilmette, Illinois, 1954.

The Power of Unity

Letter to the Continental Boards of Counsellors. International Teaching Centre. Bahá'í World Centre: Haifa, Israel, 5 December 1988.

Lights of Guidance: A Bahá'í Reference File. Compiled by Helen Hornby. Bahá'í Publishing Trust: New Delhi, India, 1983, revised 1994.

Ocean: Free Software Library of the World's Religious Literature. Developed by Chad Jones. < www.bahai-education.org/ocean >

Paris Talks. 'Abdu'l-Bahá. Bahá'í Publishing Trust: London, 1995 edition.

Portals to Freedom. Howard Colby Ives. George Ronald Publishing: Oxford, England, 1937, 1990 edition.

The Power of Unity: Beyond Prejudice and Racism. Compiled by Bonnie Taylor, National Race Unity Committee. Bahá'í Publishing Trust, Wilmette, Illinois, 1986.

The Promise of World Peace. Universal House of Justice. Bahá'í World Centre: Haifa, Israel, October 1985.

The Promised Day Is Come. Shoghi Effendi. Bahá'í Publishing Trust: Wilmette, Illinois, 1980.

The Promulgation of Universal Peace. Talks by 'Abdu'l-Bahá during His visit to the U.S. and Canada in 1912. Bahá'í Publishing Trust: Wilmette, Illinois, 1982 edition.

Ridván 1996 Message to the Bahá'ís of North America. The Universal House of Justice. Bahá'í World Centre: Haifa, Israel, 1996.

Ridván 2000 Message to the Bahá'ís of the World. The Universal House of Justice. Bahá'í World Centre: Haifa, Israel, 2000.

Selections from the Writings of 'Abdu'l-Bahá. Translated by a Committee at the Bahá'í World Centre and Marzieh Gail. Bahá'í World Centre: Haifa, Israel, 1978, 1982 printing.

The Sneetches. Theodor Geisel, a.k.a. Dr. Seuss. Random House Books: New York, 1961.

Tablet to The Hague. Originally *Lawh-i-Hague,* 1919. 'Abdu'l-Bahá. Authorized translation included in a memorandum from the Research Department at the Bahá'í World Center, February, 2002. < http://bahai-library.com/abdulbaha_lawh_hague_bwc >

Tablets of Bahá'u'lláh Revealed after the Kitáb-i-Aqdas. Translated by Habíb Taherzadeh with the assistance of a Committee at the Bahá'í World Centre. Bahá'í World Centre: Haifa, Israel, 1978.

Traditional Practices in Africa. The Universal House of Justice. Bahá'í World Centre: Haifa, Israel, 16 December 1998.

The World Order of Bahá'u'lláh. Selected Letters by Shoghi Effendi. Bahá'í Publishing Trust: Wilmette, Illinois, 1938, 1974 rev. ed., 1982 reprint.

WORKS BY THE SAME AUTHOR

www.UnityWorksStore.com

Some books also available from: www.BahaiBookStore.com, (800) 999-9019
and Special Ideas: www.bahairesources.com, (800) 326-1197

Check our website for high-quality, low-cost, easy-to-use Bahá'í resources. Download PowerPoint firesides, Five Year Plan study guides, children's class materials, Bahá'í mini ads, and much more!

Activity Books for Bahá'í Children's Classes

This series of easy-to-use teacher's guides is filled with fun, hands-on, kid-tested learning activities designed for ages 8-12. A useful resource for Bahá'í summer and winter schools, Holy Day programs, academic classes and weekend retreats. The activities were developed and tested in the field, in response to the needs of teachers and children, and have been used successfully in multiple settings over many years. Each book includes detailed lessons, copy-ready student handouts, song sheets, craft instructions and more!

"Your curriculum is the best I've seen to teach kids about the Faith. I love it!! They aren't being taught principles, they are investigating, exploring, and owning the principles."
— **Sue Walker, PhD**

Bahá'í Children's Retreats (A Complete Planning Guide)

Want to plan an unforgettable Bahá'í activity for children ages 8-12, but don't know where to begin? This retreat planning guide covers the following topics:

- Sponsorship, Schedules, Forms
- Teachers, Facility, Finances, Publicity
- Registration, Materials, Menus
- Orientation, Children's Performance
- Outdoor Activities and more!

Also included are medical release forms, recipes, a planning checklist and a graduation certificate—everything you need to organize a successful children's retreat. This planning guide is the perfect companion to the activity books on each theme.

"This retreat was life changing. You feel a renewal of passion for educating children!"
— **Lynn Haug, parent**

Bahá'í Public Speaking (Teacher's Guide with Nine Workshops)

This practical, easy-to-use teacher's guide contains nine hands-on workshops on Bahá'í public speaking. It is designed to equip youth, adults and children with the skills and confidence needed to become more effective teachers of the Faith. Participants will learn to speak with clarity and conviction—from the kitchen table to the conference hall. Be prepared for home visits, devotional meetings, fireside talks, direct teaching campaigns and public discourse. Great for junior youth groups, youth workshops and campus clubs!

This training manual can be used in conjunction with Ruhi Book 6.
It comes complete with copy-ready student handouts. Each lesson includes:

- Warm-up activities
- Speaking tips
- Practice exercises
- Homework assignment

"Fabulous! I'm very glad that you're publishing this, and I hope it is widely circulated!"
– Erica Toussaint

Once to Every Man and Nation (Stories About Becoming a Bahá'í)

A great gift for seekers, this book brings together 37 heartwarming stories of how people became Bahá'ís. The contributors to *Once to Every Man and Nation* come from all over North America and represent a wide variety of cultural, racial, social and ethnic backgrounds. Young and old, black and white, each with a different experience of life, their very diversity demonstrates the universal appeal of the Bahá'í teachings.

"Will be enjoyed by many believers...thoroughly recommend it."
– Bahá'í Reviewing Panel of the United Kingdom

Bahá'í Mini Ads

Thirty small print ads for use with local media campaigns. The series is designed to complement our Bahá'í teaching efforts by creating greater awareness and positive interest in the Faith. It includes basic Bahá'í beliefs and principles, short quotations from the Bahá'í Writings, offers of free literature, an invitation to the core activities, and an invitation to join the Bahá'í community. The file is in Microsoft Word format so it is easy to insert local contact information.

"These will surely boost teaching efforts in all communities that use them!"
– Dale Eng

PowerPoint Firesides on the Bahá'í Faith

 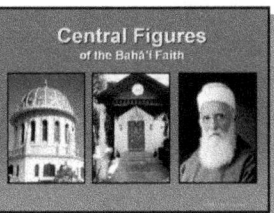  

(1)
**The Bahá'í Faith:
An Introduction***

(2)
**Central Figures
of the Bahá'í Faith**

(3)
**The Proclamation
of Bahá'u'lláh**

(4)
**The Power
of Unity**

These colorful slide shows are designed to introduce the Bahá'í Faith. They offer an overview of the Faith: its Central Figures, purpose, core beliefs and teachings, photographs of its World Center, Houses of Worship, and scenes from Bahá'í community life. The programs have been used to effectively share the Bahá'í teachings in churches, classrooms, public libraries and community firesides.

- Perfect for high school and university students
- Ideal for projecting in large group settings
- Can also be used with a laptop one-on-one

* Also available in French and Spanish

What People Are Saying

"I don't know if the presentation could have gone any better!...This was one of the most amazing teaching experiences I've ever had!" — **Charisse Johnson, student**

"... a wonderful conclusion to our study of world faiths...it makes for a great end of semester presentation." — **Steve Deligan, high school religion teacher**

"...a fantastic presentation...very understandable...excellent to use for youth."
— **Seth Walker, youth**

"A wonderful trilogy for humans everywhere to learn from." — **Beth Shevin, seeker**

"...a great success tonight in Australia...the Baha'is were very pleased with their professional quality." — **Nancy Watters, traveling teacher**

"...straight-forward...high-quality...a wonderful introduction to the Teachings"
— **Shannon Javid, Regional Bahá'í Council member**

"Very respectful and professional. Job well done!" — **Warren Odess-Gillett**

 **Download from: www.UnityWorksStore.com**

Starting a Bahá'í-Inspired Academic School

This booklet presents basic guidelines and suggestions for those considering the establishment of a Bahá'í-inspired academic school. It provides a useful framework for organizing critical tasks and decisions, utilizing a detailed checklist with hundreds of practical tips.

Escuela de las Naciones (School of the Nations)

Description with color photographs of a Bahá'í-inspired K-6 elementary school established in Puerto Rico in 1991. This monograph provides an overview of the establishment and functioning of the private, non-profit, competency-based school, including the students, facilities, classroom design, curriculum, instructional methods and materials, system of evaluation, schedule, integration of the arts, and service.

Service: Heart of the Curriculum for a Global Civilization

This monograph considers the significance of service to mankind as a central organizing principle for our educational endeavors, and recommends practical strategies for systematically integrating service into the daily life and culture of our schools.

Principles into Practice

Workshop and compilation of Bahá'í Writings on education. This resource is offered as a tool for educators who wish to put Bahá'í principles into practice in their classrooms. Detailed step-by-step instructions for conducting the workshop are presented, and copy-ready student handouts are included. The workshop complements Ruhi Book 3 training and is appropriate for Bahá'ís and friends of the Faith.

Needs Assessment Survey to Determine the Training Requirements of International Bahá'í Traveling Teachers

This doctoral thesis details the training needs of personnel on international service projects. The survey of 200 returned volunteers and Bahá'í Institutions in the 81 countries they visited, was done under the auspices of the U.S. Bahá'í International Goals Committee. The study focuses on cross-cultural communication, critical incidents, training and materials design.

The Power of Unity

List of Activities by Chapter

Opening Activities   Page
    1. Unity bingo (ice-breaker) 14
    2. Room mixer (ice-breaker) 14
    3. Group match (ice-breaker) 14
    4. Venn diagram (ice-breaker) 15-16
    5. Getting to know you (ice-breaker) 17-18
    6. Videos (introducing the theme) 19
    7. Jigsaw puzzles (social activity) 19
    8. Group singing (instructions, song sheets, musical scores) 143-144, 161-178

Lesson 1: The Power of Unity
    1. God Is One (song) 22
    2. Introduction to the theme (teacher talk) 22
    3. Definitions of "unity" and "disunity" (pairs brainstorm) 22
    4. Unity is /Disunity is (reading with questions) 23, 29
    5. Pantomime (movement activity) 23
    6. The benefits of unity (demonstrations) 23-26
        A. Bundle of sticks 23
        B. Heavy chair 24
        C. Donkey tug o' war 24
        D. Hot and cold 24
        E. Shoe demo 25
        F. Word puzzle 26
        G. Summary 26
    7. Unity (reading with student questions) 26, 30
    8. So powerful (memory quote) 27
    9. Closing questions (review) 28
  10. Si Estamos Juntos (song) 28
  11. Lanyards (craft) 28, 50

Lesson 2: Unity in Diversity
    1. Memory quote (review) 34
    2. Similarities and differences (brainstorming and movement activity) 34-35
    3. Leaves of one tree (class discussion) 35
    4. Unity in diversity (reading with student questions) 35, 40

The Power of Unity

List of Activities by Chapter (continued)

   5. Musical demonstration (singing) 36
   6. The eye (felt lesson) 36, 41-45
   7. Machines in motion (pantomime and class discussion) 36-37
   8. Unity in diversity (small group discussion) 38, 46
   9. Regard ye not (memory quote) 38
10. One Planet, One People (song) 39
11. Craft activities 39, 47-54
     A. Flowers of one garden (cut-and-paste collage) 48-49
     B. Lanyards (braiding with flat plastic lacing) 50
     C. Leaf laminates (leaf arrangement and laminating with hot iron) 51-53
     D. Diversity streamers (hanging decoration with ribbon and tin can) 54

Lesson 3: The Colors We Are
   1. Memory quotes (review) 58
   2. Skin color (demonstration and discussion) 58-59
   3. Colors of our world (teacher talk with pictures) 59
   4. How we got our skin color (story with questions) 60, 62
   5. Class features chart (groups investigate and report back) 60, 63-64
   6. Hooray for skin (poem) 61, 65
   7. Good Neighbors (song) 61
   8. Personal poster (write, trace, paint, cut and paste) 61, 66-69

Lesson 4: Overcoming Prejudice
   1. Memory quotes (review) 74
   2. Bridges and barriers (brainstorming and word wall) 74-75
   3. Prejudice (class discussion) 75
   4. The Sneetches (poem with comprehension questions) 76, 81
   5. Putdowns (brainstorming and class discussion) 76-77
   6. Personal stories (small group sharing) 77, 82
   7. Put-ups (brainstorming and discussion) 78
   8. Dealing with putdowns and prejudice (reading) 78, 83
   9. Name it, claim it (worksheet and skits) 78, 84
10. The Black Rose (story with questions) 79, 85-86
11. Chocolate Roses (craft) 79, 87
12. Creating unity (role plays) 79, 159
13. Barriers into bonds (felt lesson) 80, 88-94
14. In the sight of God (memory quote) 80
15. What Mankind Has to Learn (song) 80
16. Circle of unity (visualization) 80, 95

The Power of Unity

List of Activities by Chapter (continued)

Additional Activities

Warm-ups
1. Birthday line-up 99
2. Link-ups 99
3. Human knot 99

Craft Projects
1. Rainbow chain 100
2. Paper people 100
3. Ribbon of hearts 100
4. Chalk mural 101
5. Leaves of one tree 101-102
6. Pigment posters 103

Outdoor Games
1. Tug of peace 104
2. Cooperative musical chairs 104-105
3. Freeze dance 105
4. Beach ball volley 105
5. Loop-de-hoop 106
6. Lava island 106
7. All aboard 106
8. Fingertip touchdown 107
9. Trust walk 107
10. Electric fence 108
11. Centipede 108

Skits and Demonstrations
1. Colors of the heart 110
2. What's in a name 110
3. Garden flowers 111
4. Cooperation skit.. 112-113
5. The human body 112, 114-119
6. Seven candles of unity 120-121

Further Reading and Research 122-123

The Power of Unity

List of Activities by Chapter (continued)

Children's Performance

1. Various songs, memory quotes, presentation of crafts 125-140, 143-146
2. Stick and bundle (demo) 130
3. Heavy chair (skit) 130
4. Unity in diversity (short talk) 131
5. Row your boat (musical demo) 130
6. Opening prayer (reading) 132
7. The eye (felt lesson) 133
8. Hooray for Skin (poem) 134
9. Colors of our world (demonstration) 131
10. How we got our skin color (short play) 131, 135-136
11. Barriers into bonds (felt lesson) 137
12. We can build a beautiful world (mini-opera) 138

Music

1. Instructions for group singing 161-163
2. Song sheet 164-165
3. Musical scores 166-177
   A. Glorious Day 167
   B. God Is One / Dios Es Uno 168-169
   C. Good Neighbors 170
   D. Hawaiian Unity Song 171
   E. I Am One Voice 172
   F. Oh, Bahá'u'lláh 173
   G. One, Planet, One People 174
   H. Si Estamos Juntos 175
   I. What Mankind Has to Learn 176
   J. We Can Build a Beautiful World 177-178

Closing and Follow-up Activities 179-182

The Power of Unity – Index

Index of Activities by Category

(Note: Some items are listed in more than one category.)

Arts and Crafts | Page

- Chalk mural (freehand drawing) 101
- Children's performance (project presentations) 129
- Chocolate roses (mixed-media sculpture) 79, 87
- Diversity streamers (hanging decoration with ribbon and tin can) 54
- Flowers of one garden (cut-and-paste collage) 48-49
- Folder decorations (draw, cut and paste) 13
- Lanyards (braiding with flat plastic lacing) 28, 50
- Leaf laminates (leaf arrangement and laminating with hot iron) 51-53
- Leaves of one tree (trace, cut and write) 101-102
- Paper people (draw, cut and paste) 100
- Personal poster (write, trace, paint, cut and paste) 61, 66-69
- Pigment posters (cut and paste) 103
- Rainbow chain (cut and paste) 100
- Ribbon of hearts (draw, cut and paste) 100

Brainstorming, Questions and Discussion

- Black Rose (story with questions) 79, 85-86
- Bridges and barriers (brainstorming and word wall) 74-75
- Definitions of "unity" and "disunity" (pairs brainstorm) 22
- How we got our skin color (story with questions) 60, 62
- Leaves of one tree (class discussion) 35
- Machines in motion (pantomime and class discussion) 36-37
- Personal stories (small group sharing) 77, 82
- Prejudice (class discussion) 75
- Putdowns (brainstorming and class discussion) 76-77
- Put-ups (brainstorming and class discussion) 78
- Similarities and differences (brainstorming and movement activity) 34-35
- Skin color demo (demonstration and discussion) 58-59
- Sneetches (poem with questions) 76, 81
- Unity (reading with student questions) 26, 30
- Unity in diversity (reading with student questions) 35, 40
- Unity in diversity (reading with student questions) 38, 46
- Unity is /Disunity is (reading with questions) 23, 29

The Power of Unity – Index

Demonstrations
Donkey tug of war (cooperation) 24
Heavy chair (power of unity) 24, 130
Hot and cold (cooperation) 24
Musical demonstration (sameness, diversity, unity) 36, 130
Shoe demo (interdependence) 25
Similarities and differences (brainstorming and movement activity) 34-35
Skin color (demonstration and discussion) 58-59
Stick and bundle (strength in unity) 23, 130
Word puzzle (power of unity) 26

Dramatizations
Colors of the heart (skit) 110
Cooperation (skit) 112-113
Creating unity (role plays) 79, 159
Donkey tug of war (skit) 24
Garden flowers (skit) 111
Heavy chair (skit) 24, 130
How we got our skin color (short play) 131, 135-136
Machines in motion (pantomime) 36-37
Name it, claim it (worksheet with role plays) 78, 84
Pantomime of unity and disunity (creative movement) 23
Seven candles of unity (dramatic reading) 120-121
Stick and bundle (demo) 23, 130
We Can Build a Beautiful World (mini-opera) 138, 177-178

Felt Lessons
Barriers into bonds (overcoming prejudice) 80, 88-94, 137
The eye (unity is not sameness) 36, 41-45, 133
The human body (unity in diversity) 112, 114-119

Games and Puzzles
All aboard 106
Beach ball volley 105
Centipede 108
Cooperative musical chairs 104-105

Electric fence	108
Freeze dance	105
Human knot	99
Jigsaw puzzles	19
Lava island	106
Loop-de-hoop	106
Fingertip touchdown	107
Trust walk	107
Tug of peace	104
Unity bingo	14
What's in a name (personal acronyms)	110

Ice-breakers and Warm-ups

Birthday line-up	99
Getting to know you	17-18
Group match	14
Human knot	99
Jigsaw puzzles	19
Link-ups	99
Room mixer	14
Unity bingo	14
Venn diagram	15-16

Memory Quotes and Prayers

All quotations	145-146
Children's performance	128-129
In the sight of God there is no difference	80
Memory quote (review)	34, 58, 74
Opening prayer (children's performance)	132
Regard ye not one another as strangers	38
So powerful is the light of unity	27

Miscellaneous and Audio-Visual

Circle of unity (visualization)	80, 95
Colors of our world (talk with pictures)	59, 131
Unity in diversity (student presentation)	131
Videos (introducing the theme of unity)	19
What's in a name (personal acronyms)	110

The Power of Unity – Index

Music

Children's performance	128
Instructions for group singing	161-163
List of songs	166
1. Glorious Day	167
2. God Is One / Dios Es Uno	22, 168-169
3. Good Neighbors	61, 170
4. Hawaiian Unity Song	171
5. I Am One Voice	172
6. Oh, Bahá'u'lláh	173
7. One Planet, One People	39, 174
8. Si Estamos Juntos	28, 175
9. We Can Build a Beautiful World (mini-opera)	138, 177-178
10. What Mankind Has to Learn	80, 176
Musical demonstration (sameness, diversity, unity)	36, 130
Musical scores	165-175
Song sheet	143-144, 163-164

Readings, Stories and Poems

Black Rose	79, 85-86
Dealing with putdowns and prejudice	78, 83
Further Reading and Research	122-123
Hooray for skin	61, 65, 134
How we got our skin color	60, 62
Seven candles of unity	120-121
Sneetches	76, 81
Unity	26, 30
Unity in diversity	35, 40
Unity is /Disunity is	23, 29

Review

Memory quotes	34, 58, 74
Questions about unity	28
Summary of the benefits of unity	26

Worksheets

Class features chart (investigating our colors)	60, 63-64
Name it, claim it (responding to biased remarks)	78, 84

www.ingramcontent.com/pod-product-compliance
Lightning Source LLC
Chambersburg PA
CBHW080539170426
43195CB00016B/2610